Recruiting 101

MAURA- YOU WERE THE BEST STUDENT
BROADCASTER/RECRUITER I HAD IN 40
YEARS AT UCLA AND WE WERE SO LUCKY
YOU DECIDED TO COME + YOUR SISTER
FOLLOWED. YOUR ACCOMPLISHMENTS ARE
TREMENDOUS + SO PROUD OF YOU + YOUR
FAMILY. THIS BOOK NEEDED YOU TO
BE INCLUDED + MY LIFE HAS BEEN SO
MUCH BETTER BECAUSE OF WHAT YOU HAVE
DONE WITH YOURS.

Michael Sondheimer

Recruiting
101

AN INNOVATIVE GUIDE FOR COACHES, PARENTS
& FUTURE COLLEGE RECRUITS

Michael Sondheimer

ISBN: 1508513880
ISBN 13: 9781508513889

Table of Contents

Cover Photo of UCLA's 1978 National Championship Women's Basketball
Team courtesy of UCLA Sports Information

Acknowledgements

This book would not be possible without the teachings and support of former UCLA Senior Associate Athletic Director Judith Holland along with the lessons I have learned from my wife Barbara over the past 24 years. Holland hired me in 1977 as the nation's first women's college athletics promotions director. She then added sports information and fundraising responsibilities as I grew in my position until I found my true passion and success in athletic recruiting. My wife has contributed more to that success than she realizes by helping me develop skills as a husband, father and overall person.

I want to thank the coaches, staff members, student assistants, parents and recruits whom I've worked with over the years. They have been trusting of my different recruiting ideas and philosophy from the most common practices at the time. I learned how much I loved the recruiting process and that I could do the job after participating in an athletic department recruiting educational clinic taught in the early 1980s by former Stanford Hall of Fame basketball player and lecturer George Selleck. Former UCLA football recruiting coordinator Bill Rees and his successor, Randy Taylor, taught me methods that could be redefined for all sports.

In my new department recruiting position, former UCLA Athletic Director Peter Dalis asked me in 1984 to begin working with men's basketball along with the other sports outside of football. This meant running the recruiting section at Pauley Pavilion home basketball games, participating in campus visits and designing new strategies for landing national recruits.

Then through the support of football Coach Terry Donahue, the recruiting system I developed became department-wide. Athletic Director Dan Guerrero succeeded Dalis in the early 2000s and saw the combined sport system advantages. He let me continue the recruiting operation until my retirement in June of 2013.

Our son, Jeffrey, loved going to the UCLA sports events and especially post-season play in basketball and other sports. Both Barbara and Jeffrey started attending over 30 events a year as active participants in the recruiting process knowing I would work 24-7 to help the coaches succeed. My brother, Eric, helped push me to want to be the best in my field because he has been so successful as a Los Angeles Times sports reporter. He is well respected in the media side of sports. We were able to keep our jobs separate even though our paths crossed many times in the recruiting process and his drive and peer respect has been an inspiration.

Finally, I have so much appreciation and respect for legendary former UCLA basketball Coach John Wooden, who had a huge impact on my life. Also I want to thank Fred Eisenhammer, who is a marvelous copy editor on this book.

I have always loved the challenge that recruiting provides on a daily basis. I hope that the uniqueness of this book will help coaches, parents and recruits achieve recruiting success.

Prologue

"Recruiting 101" is designed to be an innovative book that improves the recruiting techniques of college coaches working in this demanding process. Additionally, it is written to teach parents and their teenagers how to best maneuver within the challenging college recruiting rules for future athletic scholarships.

There are recommendations in each chapter that can teach coaches trying to improve their programs nationally through a more effective recruiting approach. There are tips in each chapter that can provide parents/recruits with a platform to find the right college and scholarship to continue the playing career after the high school level. The book provides a blueprint into what coaches can utilize to make the final scholarship decisions winning ones and for recruits and parents to better select the right level of college to attend.

Whether it is football, basketball or a smaller Olympic sport or competing within the National Collegiate Athletic Association (NCAA) or National Association of Intercollegiate Athletics (NAIA), the "TEAM" recruiting system introduced within the book works well for university athletic success.

Recruiting success is best achieved by developing positive relationships within a college program that can be translated to recruits and parents. This process is enhanced by using the "Circle of Influence" as explained within the book. This provides the best chance for the future student-athlete and parents to find the best overall program.

The "Circle of Influence," combined with the "ABC-123" Recruiting Matchup System as explained in the book, is a major advantage for a college program to land a top recruit. Utilizing the different recruiting techniques can work for any college sport. This gives a coach the edge that he/she needs to persuade the recruit and family to attend his/her university.

From a parent and recruit standpoint, the book provides realistic guidelines for the athlete to determine the level of the college program to be able to best compete successfully. This means not only athletically, but performing well in the classroom. The book provides a better understanding of how recruiting takes place and scholarships are offered.

Colleges want to win on all levels. They usually recruit multiple people for the same spot/position, hoping to land their No. 1 choice. However, schools have to find someone to fit/fulfill their needs each year. Parents need to know where their son or daughter stands in that process so they have options too. Scholarship amounts differ by sport and divisions, based on "head count" vs. "equivalency" sports. There are many variables to consider. This includes receiving financial aid instead of athletic aid, or being a walk-on non-scholarship athlete at a higher level program, which are explained.

"Recruiting 101" will help parents and their future college student-athletes ask the right questions and what to look for in the process. Parents and recruits can learn the differences between equivalency and head count sports and number of scholarships available per sport. It is important to utilize the "College Comparison Chart" in the book, which can work for parents/recruits at all levels and make for a more intelligent final choice.

"Recruiting 101" is designed to help parents and recruits select the "right" college. Use the information in the book as a teaching tool/blueprint to obtain a better recruiting outcome as parents/teenagers narrow this potentially life-changing college decision. Everyone can win in recruiting by reading and using the information provided.

The NCAA has been the collegiate organization that has tried to set a level playing field in its recruiting rules. Publications such as the "NCAA Guide for College-Bound Student-Athletes"[1] is a keeper for anyone involved in the recruiting process. "Recruiting 101" utilizes current NCAA rules and academic requirements to go with proven recruiting techniques in providing a blueprint over 10 chapters that should have relevance.

---

1 www.ncaa.org web site

CHAPTER 1

You Don't Get a Second Chance
to Make a First Impression

Recruiting is primarily about building and establishing positive re-lationships. Most coaches and colleges don't get a second chance to make a memorable first impression with a top recruit and his/her parents.

First impressions can come as early as the seventh, eighth or ninth grade or as late as the official campus visit during the senior year for late-developing recruits. The same also applies to less-recruited athletes as they try to sort out possible colleges to attend when they are not the top prospects.

Sometimes recruits and their parents don't want to make an early schol-arship decision until closer to National Letter of Intent time (November of the senior year for most sports/February for a limited number of sports such as football. April is the late signing period for fall sports). This is acceptable as long as the college still has scholarship money available. However, the lat-est trend is for coaches to offer scholarships earlier and earlier (now some sports in ninth or tenth grade) and want final decisions made usually before the senior year begins in most sports.

The top-ranked colleges in each sport try to sway the best recruits into making an early decision. Meanwhile, the coaches of the middle level colleges are also offering scholarships earlier in an effort to have the next level of recruit to commit to their schools. Their hope is to commit the recruit before he/she develops to the extent that the top college may want them later. It means parents need to have a better understanding of the recruiting process than ever before. That is why the first college impression becomes so important.

Coaches: Whenever you go out to evaluate prospects or you are on your campus and know recruits are going to visit, wear clothing with your college name or logo on it. You want to send a message that you have pride in where you work. You want parents, recruits and anyone else around an event or on your campus to know your affiliation immediately.

The same applies to your first home visit or off-campus contact. Parents and recruits don't wear suits or formal dresses around their house. From my previous home visit experience, you make a family nervous and self-conscious if you are overdressed for a home visit. Wear a school polo shirt or logo lightweight jacket or something casual and comfortable that represents your university. You want to portray the image that you are someone that parents can respect as the future coach of their son or daughter. This includes making contact at a restaurant or at the high school.

How you dress could be almost as important as what you say and how you act. In one home visit (we lost the recruit), the coach went into an affluent home in the heat of summer wearing a sports jacket and tie while the parents and recruit were dressed in shorts and T-shirts. It was very uncomfortable for the family (I was in a school logo polo shirt and slacks).

I knew after leaving the home that there was no chance of the recruit committing to our college. The family wasn't comfortable with the head coach, starting with the first impression.

Do your homework and prepare for the first contact, regardless of where the meeting takes place, in the same way as you would prepare your team to compete. It works.

First Correspondence: If you evaluate a recruit with the potential for a full scholarship and you are writing your first letter, do it handwritten to make a major first impression. Most schools now do a form email or mailed letter to a recruit to fill out a biography form or to introduce the head coach within NCAA rules.

Separate yourselves from your competition with not only a handwritten note, but handwrite the recruit's address on the envelope you send. Promotional stationery within the NCAA rules that showcases the success of the overall athletic program is best to use. Having your own personal athletic stationery is nice for later on, but you should start with "selling" your overall college and not just your program. Too many coaches worry about the "I" and forget the "TEAM," which is the overall program that you are part of and should be able to represent in a positive way.

Respond to Everything: My philosophy is to respond to every letter, email, phone call, fax, text, etc. within NCAA rules and guidelines. Even if the information is limited or shows the recruit probably can't compete for you, always make sure there is a response.

You never know when that recruit will have an all-star younger brother or sister. You don't necessarily know if the parents or grandparents are donors to your university or had other siblings attend your school. You may not know if the recruit could be club mates or best friends with someone you really want to recruit and could help you succeed in the process.

There is way too much to lose by throwing the correspondence away or "blowing off" the phone call. It is so much easier to respond. While I was involved day-to-day in recruiting, we signed some incredible recruits by taking the time to respond to the first contact or phone call. The positive first impression always helps.

Suggestions for a Positive First Impression

1. Separate yourself from the competition with a handwritten note with biography form (for younger top recruits-email is too common)
2. Early phone call to his/her HS/club coach where you get recruit to call you back (should be done by head coach)
3. Make sure the recruit you want sees you are there evaluating him/her competing by wearing school logo shirt/jacket
4. Utilizing your current athletes that may be former teammates and their parents to let recruit know of your interest within NCAA rules
5. Getting desired recruit to visit your campus unofficially/sports camp

Coaches' Most Important Recruiting Tools for Making a Positive First Impression

I.   Athletic Department Website, University Website, Site Videos, Facebook, Twitter, Instagram, YouTube, Current Social Media

II.   Individual Sport Websites Constantly Updated/Twitter Event Updates

III.   Unofficial Visits/Junior Days (stationery, envelopes, materials for packets)

IV.   Preptracker/Google Alerts (tracking your top recruits early)

V.   Videos/Virtual Facility/Campus Tours/Make Campus Tour Unique

VI.   Communication-Mailings, Emails, Parents vs. Recruits, Coaches, NCAA Guide for College-Bound Student-Athletes, "Circle of Influence"

VII.   Athletic Department working as one "TEAM"—PR, Marketing, Academics, Fundraising, Weight Room, Sports Medicine

VIII. University Staff Supporting Athletics—General Tours, Materials, Welcome Days, Dorms Support, Orientations, Chancellor/President, Etc.

IX.   Showcasing your Campus Location—Attractions, Weather, Community

X.   Intangibles in Recruiting Process–What is recruit's No. 1 key for commitment?

Parents/Recruits: Most college coaches now recruit primarily at major club events and showcases, in addition to their own individual sports camps over high school games/events. Sports have their own individual NCAA recruiting periods when coaches can do in-person evaluations or make in-person contact.

Coaches are very selective in what events they attend and try to maximize their recruiting time away from their own teams. Budgets may be an issue for some smaller sports, so the coaching staff wants to make its recruiting time out productive. They like to see as many potential recruits as possible at one location. You want to have your biographical information available for the colleges you are most interested in to make a positive first impression.

The coaches are limited by NCAA rules as to when they can watch you play/compete or talk to you in person. They can't make in-person off-campus contact with you or your parents until after 11th grade in most sports. However, with updated NCAA rules, beginning in 11th grade in most sports, you can receive phone calls and text messages to go with email or written correspondence. The coaches can't have any correspondence with a recruit while he/she is participating in a multi-day event until event completion (Division I is the most restrictive).

My best parent event recruiting advice is to stay away from the college coaches of the schools you are interested in. This is because the only likely time he/she may be able to talk is after the event is completed and your teenager is released (provided it is permissible in that sport under NCAA rules for your son or daughter to be contacted). In some sports, a coach can only watch summer events without any contact, like basketball, for example. There are a few exceptions, but most coaches just evaluate recruits at events.

Video is the best current alternative if you can't be seen in person to showcase your skills for the colleges you are most interested in (parents must be realistic in what level of competition your son/daughter can really compete).

–**Videos:** Should be 3 to 5 minutes in length (works best if taken from your sport competition or doing skill drills) that highlights why a college would think you are of scholarship caliber. Speed/quickness/athleticism/power are optimal in every sport, so show something where you have movement whether land or water. You can place the video on YouTube or another high school recruiting website, but make sure you provide the coach with a direct link to make it easier to find.

The video should highlight strengths and key skills that a college would be looking for in that sport. Show offensive/defensive plays, shooting/ball-handling, baseline-volleys-serving, throwing different pitches, hitting/fielding, swimming different strokes, starting and finishing a track/cross country event, striking the ball/putting, etc. For parents, make it easy for the college to know why your son/daughter can compete at that level. **Remember**

long videos or full event competitions typically won't be watched by coaches for more than a few minutes.

–**Letters/Emails:** Sending in letters or emails as to when your son/daughter will be competing and where to watch him/her if the school is out evaluating an event is another good way of being seen at least once. Make sure the coach knows your basic biography information. For watching, let the school know your uniform/cap number or colors/logo you usually wear to make it easier to find you at an event. This matters at a club vs. high school vs. invitational or showcase.

Include a picture with your playing number or identifying features to make it easier to see you. Include your academic grade-point average, and whether you are taking honors or AP classes. Provide any standardized test scores you have, especially if the recruit is a high school junior or the summer before starting his/her senior year.

Don't forget to send basic information such as home address, cellphone, best email for you and your parents, height, weight, speed, high school/club names and coaches' names with email and phones. Include what you believe are your key scholarship qualifications and let the school know if there is an upcoming time when you will be visiting the campus unofficially. Coaches want it as simple as possible for their college to recruit you if they are interested.

–**Recruiting Services (paid):** Provide athletic videos directly to colleges around the nation, and have more value later in the process. An "all-sport" company or a smaller one that does your specific sport (usually videos, plus a biography sheet) aren't necessary if you can't afford them. Most paid services usually don't benefit a family until the summer before the start of the senior year of high school. That is based on the Division I college choices being very limited or there is no recruiting taking place.

These recruiting services are most helpful at finding scholarships at smaller colleges and schools outside of your immediate living area. These colleges likely would not have discovered you through normal recruiting channels due to limited recruiting opportunities or lack of budget. You need to decide whether you have the finances to pay for this type of specialized service that realistically provides limited help with the better Division I schools in most sports. However, this book shows ways to do your own recruiting without the major cost to find the right college.

In today's Internet recruiting world and with so many tournaments and showcases, there are few recruiting surprises for Division I schools in any sport. It doesn't matter if you compete in a small town or at a small or even losing sport high school/club, if you have college talent, the coaches will find you.

Most sport coaches now have the ability to purchase recruiting/ rating services to help them know/evaluate recruits, so there are a lot more ways to find recruits. It is extremely rare when you see a major Division I scholarship offered where a recruit was discovered for the first time by his/her parents paying for a recruiting service (even though a lot of services claim it happened that way).

When Parents/Recruits Should Start?

1. More colleges are going to earlier offers (ninth or tenth grade). The NCAA has liberalized some recruiting rules that now allow more recruiting to take place by the start of the 11th grade school year. You can start judging your scholarship ability by what type of early reaction you receive from colleges.

2. Sending out your biography information to your top 10 colleges by the start of 9th grade is a good rule of thumb (email appears to be the easiest way and almost all schools have websites with coaches' email addresses). Sending out your recruiting information after 11th grade begins is getting late. Calling a school or sending materials after 12th grade starts has limited productivity. Even if you are a late developing recruit or you have switched sports, you are behind in the scholarship process once the senior year has begun.

3. If you are starting or performing at a high level on a club team by 9th grade or starting on varsity or a top individual club competitor by that time, you will be seen by colleges. It varies by sports as to the earliest offers, but almost every sport is now offering the best athletes by the 11th grade.

4. One important tip in sending email/regular mail is don't just send out information to the head coach. If you really like a school, read the biographies of the coaches on the website, then send not only to the head coach, but to the assistant listed as the recruiting coach or to that sport director of operations. It gives you a much better chance within NCAA rules of being looked at or at least having your information reviewed/responded to.

Parents/Recruits First Impression: Look and see if you receive a college response as a sign of mutual interest or if you are contacted first by a school that is interested in you. If your son or daughter is of major sport caliber, schools will contact you through the club or high school coach. Sometimes college coaches purchase recruiting packets at major events (especially in summer) with home addresses or email contacts as a way to make a first written contact.

If colleges aren't contacting you, then my suggestion is to send out 10 letters/emails to schools in your realistic talent range as soon as high school begins with your biography information. If the college doesn't respond, then that school isn't making a positive first impression you are looking for. Under NCAA rules, a college can at least send out its own biography form or camp information to any year recruit. You deserve some type of response if you have taken the time to contact the school. First impressions are so important and should be judged both ways.

Michael Sondheimer (left) with Nana Meriwether, who played volleyball at UCLA. She became Miss USA after graduating and is an example of a great recruiting resource for her accomplishments.

CHAPTER 2

Official & Unofficial Campus Visits

This chapter covers the essentials of making college campus visits and what to look for from the coach, parent and recruit standpoints. NCAA rules allow a recruit to take a maximum of 5 expense-paid 48-hour campus official visits during the senior year of high school (you may be able to take the visit starting in the second half of your junior year in selected sports under NCAA rules. Also the college may be able to pay for your parents to come with you in a couple of sports).

The college is allowed on an official visit to pay the expenses for the recruit's transportation, parking, meals and provide home game tickets for the recruit and parents if the family comes with the recruit (usually over a Friday to Sunday). **My advice is for a recruit to always make an official visit regardless of whether if he/she has committed to that college. More on this later.**

An unofficial visit can be taken anytime (usually 9th-11th grade) where you (your parents) pay for all of the necessary expenses to get to the college campus, including parking and meals (the school can still provide up to three complimentary home event tickets). There are limited time periods when a college athletic program can't be involved in an unofficial visit (called "Dead Periods") such as around national letter of intent time or around its NCAA sport championships or college bowl games (football). You can still visit, but the college athletic program won't be able to participate in any way.

Coaches: Guidelines for providing the most successful official visits:

1. Prepare a standard 48-hour itinerary in advance with your staff to include what you would like covered during the visit. It can be utilized as a template for all official visits. This would include time with the head coach, campus tour, academic meeting, your athletic hall of fame, weight room session, sports medicine/training room/nutrition, meeting with your sport coordinator or athletic director, special academic/career/campus VIP meeting, projected meals, campus housing, transportation/local hotel and what you think is the single most important intangible in selling your campus.

2. Encourage parents to attend on the official visit, especially if the recruit made an unofficial visit and didn't have the parents with him/her. Make sure your itinerary has combined activities so parents can feel the same experience **(many parents in today's recruiting are very active in the lives of their sons or daughters and want to feel a major part of the final college decision).**

    This is especially important on the campus tour, the academic meeting and the session with the head coach (I recommend the head coach have a separate meeting with just the recruit if the parents are on the official visit). In sports where the NCAA allows for you to pay for the parents, always do it and make sure they can come to campus from anyplace in the world.

3. The finalized itinerary should be emailed in advance to both the recruit and the parents (even if they aren't coming) so they can see how organized and professional the coaching staff is in the recruiting process.

    Parents want to feel comfortable with the visit, especially if there is a flight or hotel involved. Providing this information in advance (used to be required by NCAA rules) is a major plus in the process. Most schools just communicate basic information with the recruit, but parents should be aware of all aspects of the visit process (see the "Circle of Influence").

4. Once the itinerary is finalized, then always meet with your full college team in advance (including redshirts, transfers, managers). Too many schools bypass the full team meeting to just meet with their team captains or the visit host for the recruit. That is a big mistake.

   Everyone on your team should be aware of/participate in the official visits. The visits are much more productive with fewer problems when the whole team hears what the head coach expects and wants. Also recruits and parents like to see the interaction involving potential future teammates and not just an individual or two as the decision-making process takes place. Think of the visit as a competition where you would deliver the recruiting scouting report for your team before you competed.

5. Schedule at least one meal at the resident halls (dorms) since that is where the recruit will likely be staying during the school year. This can be at "training table" with the team or where the student-athletes eat in the off-season or where you believe is the most social campus location that provides great interaction with general students (may be with a wide screen television to watch a road sports event to show school spirit or a recreation hot spot).

6. Try to have one meal at the home of the head coach or top assistant coach that lives in the geographic area to showcase family and local life. It is traditional that this happens in football and basketball, but it works just as well in the other sports. You are allowed to have your team there for the "occasional meal" within the NCAA rules.

   Other meals should be at your high priority restaurants. They should be part of your marketing/fundraising department list so you are treated as a VIP when arriving with priority reservations and the best table. You always want to look important to the recruit and his or her family within NCAA rules.

7. Take advantage of your unlimited phone calls in the days before the official visit to engage the parents in the recruiting process (utilize the "Circle of Influence"). Ask what is important for their son or daughter to see and do on the visit. Ask if there were things at the opposition schools that the recruit/parents liked or enjoyed. Ask what are the most important factors in making the final college decision? This information should help you in personalizing the 48-hour visit and help close the deal when the visit is completed.

8. Make sure the best game ticket locations are given to your top recruits within NCAA rules. Make them feel special by their seating section. Make sure you know where the recruit will be sitting and plan if you want him/her sitting by your host or around other key recruits that can help you close. You may want to sit with the parents for most of the event if your team isn't playing.

Too many schools let the ticket office do the recruit seating. If this is an important recruit, then you should be involved in getting the type of seats you want. This is especially true at a major home football or basketball game or in your own sport if it is an important campus event.

Anything you can control in the recruiting process you want to do or at least have input in the final decision-making process. You don't want your best recruit sitting next to someone you don't plan to make a scholarship offer. Also don't sit the recruit next to another recruit who is leaning toward the rival school and could influence the recruit to go with him/her.

If it is your sport, make sure you have a redshirt, transfer, manager or an athlete you trust from another sport sit with your recruit and have a plan for the parents. You don't want to leave anything to chance and having them watch your team compete is great as long as recruiting is taking place during the event. Know where your recruit is sitting and who is seated around him/her at all times.

9. Having a combined all-sport recruiting football pre-game picnic can be a major recruiting advantage. The combined picnics work great since guys usually like females and vice-versa. It is a big advantage to have your student-athletes from all sports as part of the recruiting process within NCAA official visit rules. Having recruits and parents meet other sport significant coaches and athletes is much better than being isolated with only your team. Atmosphere is so important to recruiting visit success.

Bringing in administrators, academic personnel, key faculty and other athletic staff members to meet with recruits in a more informal setting is another plus. Escorting the recruits onto the field prior to the game to be close to the action is usually exciting for the recruits and sometimes even more for the parents. Sit the recruits together with your current student-athletes mixed in so they feel like a cohesive unit. The current student-athletes can provide introductions to other students and explain game traditions during the event.

Football weekends are the best to use for recruiting, especially if you have a strong football program. If football isn't popular at your school, then look for the best home sports event. Try to run some type of combined pre-game activity around it, especially if you can add another sport team to go with you. In the fall, it can be soccer, women's volleyball, men's water polo, women's field hockey or an exhibition basketball game. This is especially important if you don't have a football program to build a weekend around.

The quality and organization of the event are so important to impress the recruit and parents. You want to work with your marketing department to maximize crowd exposure to make the recruits feel like they are part of something special. You want recruits from the different sports sitting together as a unit and supporting a positive "TEAM" recruiting experience.

10. Always debrief your team and other staff involved after the official visit for impressions/recommendations/issues. It helps you for future recruiting, and gives you a better feel of which people do the best job in the recruiting process. Record and keep the information and discuss as a staff. If you weren't able to close the recruit on the visit, then this information should help.

Parents/Recruits: There are several keys to making the campus official visit the most productive 48 hours so you can make the best final college decision. The more information, the easier the decision.

1. If you haven't been offered a scholarship, ask if you are going to be offered a scholarship on the official visit. If you have been offered a scholarship, know there will be pressure to commit to the school on the official visit. It is best to indicate in advance that you aren't planning to make a final college decision until you go back home to talk with your family. This is especially true if you have more visits to make in the recruiting process.

2. Pick the weekend that best matches with your interest in the school. If you are someone the college really wants, then you can look at their playing schedule and go in on the weekend you want. Most fall official visits are around home football games and most winter official visits are around home men's basketball games. See when your sport practices or competes to visit.

You don't want to visit on a weekend when there is a lack of campus sports activities. You want to be around not only for your possible future teammates, but to observe how other athletes interact and enjoy the college.

3. Make sure you bring with you a list of questions not only for the head coach, but for other departments that you would be involved during the college experience. For the academic counselor—do they have my major? How does tutoring work? Is tutoring individual or group? Do I get the same help in summer school? How do student-athletes do in that major compared to regular students? Can I meet another athlete in the same major?

   For weight room—how many days a week do we lift? What other types of conditioning do we do? Are there make-up times if I have a midterm? What are the penalties for missing a day?

   For student-athletes on the team—how is the coach if we aren't winning—does he/she yell, scream, discipline, etc.? How are injuries handled? Who makes the decision on when you can play or if you have to redshirt with an injury (you can compare the answer by also asking sports medicine)? Can you live off-campus after the first year or does coach require you to be on campus all four years? Is your sport treated the same as other sports?

   Don't leave campus without your main questions being answered, so write them down and update with the answers.

4. Make sure you spend quality time in the resident halls (dorms) where you will likely be living during the school year. Too many schools keep you always at the hotel or on the run and you see the dorms for 10 to 15 minutes. That isn't enough time regardless of your sport. You want to see other dorm rooms, eating halls, study rooms, extra amenities like washer-dryer, workout room, game room, front desk, etc. Can you see yourself living there during the school year?

5. Don't leave the campus without a firm scholarship offer that can be put into writing as long as it is during the senior year with NCAA rules. If there is going to be a deadline on accepting the scholarship, get that in writing. You should also follow up by

writing back to the coach with your understanding of the scholarship offer so you have a record of it. If you don't get the scholarship offer, then move onto plan B.

You may be No. 2 or No. 4 in the order for scholarships waiting on No. 1 so you don't want to lose out if you have another school you want more. Make sure you know the recruiting deadlines. If you are not offered a scholarship, then ask the question as to where you stand. Consider your next best choice that has already made a scholarship offer if you don't want to wait.

6. Review in detail how you were treated—transportation, hotel/dorms, meals, game tickets, campus tour, academic/staff meetings, etc. You are making a life-changing decision and don't want to leave anything to chance. **Bottom line question to ask yourself: Can you visualize attending that college?**

Unofficial Visits

Coaches: All unofficial visits should be designed to come as close to an official visit as possible within the NCAA rules. This is especially important with more and more schools making scholarship offers to ninth or tenth graders. The top recruits seldom last to the senior year official visits without making a commitment in most sports.

The next level of recruits are being offered full or big scholarships now by the mid-majors hoping to snap them up early before the top division I schools get around to offering scholarships. Don't be late if you really want a recruit. You have to know what your competition is doing or you could lose out.

1. Unofficial visits now happen year round (outside of NCAA "Dead Periods"– around letters of intent, NCAA Championships or Coaches Conventions in certain sports). You need to have your program ready to provide campus and athletic facility tours when legitimate recruits and teams are

in your area. Being prepared and organized can be the difference in your success.

2. Develop a plan on how you want to have recruits greeted when they arrive on your campus and shown your athletic department if you can't be there. This is so important that the recruit can see the Athletic Department and the facilities so that the family knows if your school can meet their main needs to want to return. If you can be there, then work with the club coach or high school coach if you can't communicate directly because of NCAA rules so he/she can have a quality experience. The first impression is so important.

It is significant that the recruit can meet with you or at least one of your assistant coaches to ask questions and you should ask questions of the recruit/parents. If any of your student-athletes are around, utilize them in the process. Take advantage of your best or most reliable campus resources.

3. Very few coaches review their recruiting databases or files prior to recruits making unofficial visits to make sure their information is up to date—correct high school, club, home email, correct address, city, state, zip, cell number. If you can't be there, have someone verify the information from your computer database or printed biography sheet so you have any new information that can help you.

Track parent information too. This is such a great opportunity for recruiting success and you can never have too much information. Any small biography change that you can get now will help future recruiting and put you ahead of your opposition.

4. If you are in control of unofficial visits such as "Junior Days" or teams coming into town with strong prospects of interest, then the No. 1 thing you want to ask for is a "transcript." Coaches usually believe that anyone who is of scholarship quality can get through their admission process.

That may be the case, but with the more demanding NCAA requirements beginning for fall of 2016, it is imperative to start early in making sure your recruit has the right classes to be admitted to your college. You don't want to waste valuable time recruiting someone who can't get in or likely won't be NCAA eligible to compete.

5. Make your "Junior Days" program as close to an official visit as you can, because you may not get another chance to recruit before the college decision is made. Coaches shouldn't worry if they do "everything" for a "Junior Day" that they won't get an official visit during the senior year. There are many new things to show and do on the official visit that you can't do on the unofficial. The recruit in almost every case will visit again if you are at the top of his/her list. You have the power to insist on being one of the five official visits or no scholarship will be offered.

    The keys for a successful "Junior Day" program includes the academic meeting, the campus tour, seeing athletic facilities, seeing a dorm room and having a meal together (the dorms are preferred since it usually impresses parents), attending a top athletic event and having quality one-on-one time with the coaches.

    You definitely want to encourage parents to come for the "Junior Days" program. My belief is in combined sport and multiple "Junior Days" where you limit the total amount of recruits to 15-20 overall. You don't want more than 4 or 5 from any one sport so you can maximize your efforts.

    Having a mass recruiting "Junior Days" such as what a lot of football programs do is counterproductive from my experience, because you don't get the quality one on one time you really need with the head coach, position coach and sometimes the returning players. If you insist on doing your own sport, try to limit it to 7 to 10 prospects you would consider valuable for your team and not wide open. This allows a coaching staff to maximize time with recruits and parents. You can have multiple days around home events to cover what you need. You should learn valuable recruiting information from this experience. If you don't, then you have too many recruits at one time.

6. Sometimes I have recommended that head coaches take the No. 2 or No. 3 prospect because of a better academic record than the No. 1 recruit. His/her academic background makes it easier to predict college success in the long run. A coach may not want to hear, but each case should be evaluated. Develop an action plan related to how easily it will be to admit that recruit into your university based on being NCAA eligible and able to stay eligible at your college.

The ability for the recruit to stay college eligible is paramount because of the focus today on NCAA Graduation Rates. Bringing in the wrong recruit with a lack of academic preparation could affect the total number of scholarships available in your sport in the future. In Olympic sports, we had a policy that a recruit couldn't attend the campus "Junior Days" program and receive complimentary athletic admission tickets unless we received an advance transcript.

For football and basketball games or if you have a major home event, don't provide complimentary recruiting tickets without seeing the transcript. This allows you to best plan out the visit from an academic and recruiting standpoint to maximize the unofficial visit.

I recommend some type of an advance transcript policy for all universities to make it easier to make athletic scholarship decisions. It shows a family how serious you are about academics to go with your sport. It makes a positive impression and your job easier.

Recruits & Parents:

Every time you visit a college city for a tournament or game or to visit relatives, you should make unofficial college visits starting in eighth or ninth grade to start making comparisons. You should have your own check list of what you are looking for in a college (see chapter 6 "College Comparison Chart"). See if you can set up a campus tour and meeting in the athletic department if it is not an "NCAA Dead Period" when no recruiting can take place (you can still see the campus, but no athletic meetings).

Quick Check List of What to Bring with you for an Unofficial Visit:

A. Biography form with your background information for the coach
B. Transcript of your classes that you have taken so far and your grades
C. Schedule of upcoming club/HS games/events where you can be evaluated
D. Any short video/video website of you competing/doing drills for evaluation

Guidelines for Unofficial Visits:

1. Remember with NCAA rules, coaches can't return phone calls and maybe not emails until after the 10th grade in most sports. You may have to make all of the effort to contact the coach (better to try assistant coaches or director of operations) to see if they are available when you are able to make it to the college campus.

    If you can make the arrangements make sure the coach has your biographical/academic information before you arrive. The information makes it easier to evaluate and recruit you if you have the talent for that college to consider you for a scholarship or a preferred walk-on spot on the team.

2. Please don't waste the time and resources of a major Division I school when you are a lower Division I or Division II prospect unless you are willing to come as a walk-on without an athletic scholarship. You can still set up a university tour through the admissions office at almost any college and still walk into the athletic department and leave your information. However, don't expect the head coach to be excited if you are someone that isn't being recruited by that level of a university.

    Today, there are few surprises in any sport because of video and the Internet. Don't over-sell yourself or word can get around and hurt you with the level of university that should be recruiting you. Bottom line is to be realistic.

3. Parents should always try to come to "Junior Days" or unofficial visits to see the campus since you know best what your son or daughter really likes or needs in a college. It also means that if you trust the coach and college, you can let your son or daughter go solo for an official visit later in the recruiting process. This is especially important if financial considerations are involved. Visits are always invaluable and you want to make college comparisons by asking multiple questions before making a final decision.

    Don't pass on a senior year official campus visit if you are strongly considering a scholarship from that school just to see another college campus. This is even if you think you "know" your top school from "Junior Days" or an unofficial visit.

    You have five official expense-paid NCAA visits. I have not met a recruit or family that can't narrow down the choices to their top two or three scholarship schools. An official visit is much different than an unofficial visit because of the college being able to do so much more to showcase that school. You get to better know the student-athletes, which is so important. It makes your decision-making process easier in my opinion and you shouldn't waste another school's time and money.

CHAPTER 3

College Signing: Early vs. Late

Recruiting varies by university and by division with the actual National Letter of Intent signing period coming in either November or February when recruits reach their senior year of high school. It is very rare for a school to make an athletic scholarship offer to a recruit as young as seventh or eighth grade. Making offers to ninth and tenth graders has become a lot more common, especially in sports such as women's volleyball, women's soccer, baseball and softball. Most sports make offers to the top recruits sometime during the second semester of 10th grade or the summer before 11th grade or even after 11th grade begins.

However, for the majority of recruits, offers come in the summer before 12th grade or on the home or official visits during 12th grade. A recruit/family can make a commitment to a university anytime, but the scholarship doesn't become official until paperwork is signed in 12th grade under NCAA rules. Also a college is not supposed to put a scholarship offer into writing until the summer after the 11th grade under NCAA rules.

This chapter will explain when a recruit can actually sign scholarship papers with a college in 12th grade and more about the process from both the coach and parent/recruit standpoints.

November Senior Year Early Signing Scholarship Sports: Men's and Women's Basketball, Baseball, Golf, Gymnastics, Ice Hockey, Lacrosse, Women's Rowing, Softball, Swimming & Diving, Tennis, Track & Field/Cross Country, Volleyball, Sand Volleyball, Water Polo, Wrestling

February Senior Signing Scholarship Sports: Football (may get mid-December 3-day signing period), men's and women's soccer, men's water polo (only sports without a November signing period).

April Late Signing Period for November Senior Year Early Signing Sports.

It is estimated that more than 40,000 recruits/parents sign National Letters of Intent to attend college every year according to the "National Letter of Intent" website.[2] A letter of intent is a binding legal agreement between the college offering the athletic scholarship and the incoming student-athlete and his/her parent/legal guardian.

Because of the letter of intent rules, a parent or legal guardian must sign the letter of intent along with the recruit to bind the future student-athlete to that specific college regardless of the age of the recruit. The letter of intent is the contract part that binds the recruit to the college.

There is always a grant-in-aid financial offer sheet that goes with the letter of intent paperwork. The grant-in-aid is the financial (scholarship) part of the agreement and indicates the amount of the scholarship (full scholarship down to books offer, pending on the sport). If a recruit is graduating early from the high school (most often happens with top football prospects), then it is likely that the recruit will only sign the grant-in-aid paperwork in the fall because the letter of intent rules are specific about when you start college.

Very few recruits/families ask to have the letter of intent declared "null and void" by the National Letter of Intent committee. The most common reason for the recruit to want the letter of intent rescinded is not being admitted to that university. The most common disputed reason to "get out" of a letter of intent is because that school coach had been fired or left for another college or professional career.

It is possible for a recruit to have the letter of intent rescinded if he/she is part of an NCAA violation or if an NCAA violation is committed by the school during the recruitment process. The recruit and family are responsible for knowing the basic NCAA rules and schools should

---

2 National Letter of Intent web site www.nationalletter.org

provide "The NCAA Guide for College- Bound Student-Athletes"[3] during the recruiting process.

Coaches: Your reputation is so important because every sport community is very small. Expect parents and the coaches of their teenagers to talk regularly in the club community about almost any college and how they recruit. You want yours in a positive light because you keep your promises and recruit with integrity. If you don't tell the truth or keep your promises, expect it to be written over the Internet.

If you have a problem student-athlete situation or an athlete needs to transfer, be consistent in your actions. It helps if your university is also consistent in its actions involving athlete issues. You don't want the negative publicity from pulling a scholarship or not honoring a promised scholarship increase or not coming through with a future offer. You need to stop/deal with Internet rumors before they are treated as facts in today's social media world. Being consistent helps dissolve rumors quickly.

Recruits/Parents: You may not be 100% sure about which college to attend, but if you are sure enough, then it is worth committing for a college scholarship when you are ready. You want to sign during the early period (most sports have a November signing date) so you can enjoy your senior year of high school without the recruiting pressure. For February signing, then you can enjoy your final semester/quarter as soon as it is completed.

NCAA scholarships are one year renewable for a period of up to 5 years (15 quarters or 10 semesters of school). Under NCAA rules, you have 5 years to complete 4 years of college eligibility (you could miss one playing season for what is called a redshirt year when you don't play primarily because of injury/development reasons).

More of the bigger universities/conferences are going to guaranteed four year scholarships in the best interests of the student-athlete. Beginning in 2015-16, the top 5 conferences (Atlantic Coast Conference (ACC), Big Ten, Big 12, Pac-12, Southeastern Conference (SEC)) are going to add extra funds on top of the full athletic scholarship to cover the "Cost of Attendance" at their college as listed

---

3 NCAA.org web site

in their catalog/admission brochure (roughly $2500-$3500 extra per academic year). Also athletic scholarship aid should not be removed or reduced for sport reasons such as not performing to coach's expectations.

Several major conferences have created rules where if you compete for at least two years and leave in good academic standing (such as turning professional or having to leave for personal reasons), you can be re-admitted to the college and have your scholarship reinstated to cover educational costs until graduation. Every school has different policies. You should check with the college on your visit or via phone as to what their policies are with regard to scholarship renewal and returning to the college if you leave without completing your degree.

If you are not sure about the college, coach or scholarship offer, I suggest a couple of options that may not be popular with the schools that are recruiting you.

1. You can ask the college to maintain the early scholarship offer so you can sign late (April for November or wait till February letter of intent day for those sports). You want to see if the college has everything the same (such as the head coach/position coach returning that recruited you). You should have completed what was required academically so you are eligible to compete/or you have met any admission provision that some schools require to receive the athletic scholarship.

2. Next is to sign the letter of intent during the early period, but to get permission from the athletic director at the university (ask for it in writing) to be able to rescind the letter of intent should the head coach/recruiting coach leave the school (the most common reason a recruit wants to rescind the signing of his/ her letter of intent). This could also include an academic situation. Again check the policies and what has been done previously since a coach may not know the policy of his/her university if dismissed or if there is an academic issue.

3. Getting anything you discuss with the head coach/athletic administer in writing is vital. This is especially true if you son/daughter is not an honor student and being offered a full/partial scholarship where the coach has said the scholarship is based on being admitted to his/her university. Ask the coach to put something in writing granting your son/daughter provisional admission to the university or a letter outlining specifically what is needed to be admitted after signing the scholarship papers.

I have seen colleges deny admission later if the recruit doesn't have a great senior year athletically or if the school runs out of scholarships or the school isn't happy with the senior year grades/test scores. Also if there is a coaching change and you want to still go to the school, almost all colleges will honor the athletic scholarship.

This is especially important if the previous head coach had promised to increase your scholarship in an equivalency sport after year one (can go from books up to a full scholarship). The college may not like being questioned, but having something in writing is always the best policy for your security. Even though most coaches are trustworthy and the schools almost always follow the scholarship recommendations of their coaches, make sure you have peace of mind in writing if there are issues.

Scholarship basketball players Tracy Murray, Tyus Edney and Mitchell Butler with Sondheimer, all went onto NBA careers after college.

CHAPTER 4

Athletic Scholarships—Head Count vs. Equivalency Sports & Number Available

A thletic Scholarship Explanation: NCAA athletic scholarships are classified and limited by sport. They are divided into "head count" sports (each person given a scholarship counts as a full scholarship whether he/she receives all the funding or not) and "equivalency" sports (you can have as many athletes as you want on some type of athletic scholarship, but you can't go over that sport numerical limit).

Examples of equivalency sports are men's tennis, men's volleyball and men's water polo where each sport has fewer total athletic scholarships (4.5 is the maximum amount) than the number of athletes needed for a competition with another school. In those sports, it is likely that 10-12 athletes are receiving some type of scholarship aid, but only one or two may be on full scholarship to have enough quality athletes to field a competitive team with the limits. By comparison, men's basketball has 13 full scholarships for 13 different players when it takes five players to start a game.

When you hear the term "full ride scholarship," it means that all of your education expenses are paid (called tuition and fees); all of your living expenses on campus are paid (called room and board) and all of your course related books and materials are paid (called books scholarship).

For 2015-16, the power conferences (ACC, Big Ten, Big 12, Pac-12, and SEC) are adding in a "Cost of Attendance" expense to the full scholarship to cover the actual printed academic cost of college attendance at their schools. It is up to other individual Division I schools and sports as to whether they are going to add the extra funds. You need to check with that university and that sport as to whether the extra living-expense funds will be added.

Head count sports get everything, while equivalency sports can get some or all of the scholarship depending upon the sport and school (see athletic scholarship table). The top head count sports are football, basketball, women's volleyball, women's gymnastics and women's tennis. The top equivalency sports are baseball, softball, soccer, track & field/ cross country and swimming & diving (you have to check the NCAA list to see the total number of scholarships available in your sport).

Coaches: Regardless of the length of time left on your college contract, it is important to have a four-year recruiting plan and to make/ always have available a four-year scholarship chart of your team. It is best to try to divide your current scholarship recruiting over 4 years so you can always be recruiting new talent every year in an effort to win consistently.

It is much more difficult for the equivalency sports vs. head count sports when doing your long-range planning. Since more and more schools are offering early scholarships, you need to plan for the future. However, I always tell coaches the future is now, not a year from now. If you can get an impact recruit, take him or her now because you don't know what will happen with your team for next year.

Winning is so much more magnified in today's college athletics, so use your scholarship availability wisely. Don't pass on academically qualified prospects that can help you achieve your team goals now. Anything can happen with your team in the following year among academics, transferring, pro careers, etc.

Some colleges regularly increase scholarships each year in equivalency sports. A recruit comes in with little scholarship (such as to only cover the cost of course-related books) and if he/she excels, then the scholarship is increased each year by the coach. The NCAA says scholarships are not supposed to be awarded based on ability, but virtually 100% of equivalency scholarships are usually increased based on talent and importance to the team. It is easier to have a recruiting plan where you can show that you increase your athlete scholarships yearly.

Yearly equivalency scholarship increases help you build the best team since you are usually working with fewer scholarships than you need for a full lineup. It means you should have money available each year to recruit new talent provided you are balancing your scholarships over four years. An example would be in baseball where you need to have scholarship funds to recruit new pitchers each season since you could lose a pitcher after his junior year to the professional draft.

The head count sports are renewed each year for up to 5 years of scholarship. More and more of the "power" conferences (we recommend you do this for your impact recruits) are being guaranteed four and sometimes five year scholarships.

If you aren't in a "power" conference and you want to compete with the top schools, then you need to talk to your athletic director to guarantee scholarships. This should only be in your sport for your impact recruits. Any edge you can get in recruiting within the NCAA rules is encouraged. You have to compete on as even a playing field as possible and it may be tougher with the top colleges giving "Cost of Attendance" funds on top of the full scholarship for 2015-16.

There are many Olympic sports where your conference may be slightly different than your football or basketball conference alignment. Then you may have a blend of big schools mixed in with smaller Division I colleges. There are even a few Division II or III colleges competing with Division I schools in certain sports. If the smaller schools want to stay competitive, then they need to watch the latest trends in recruiting of the "big" schools. This is becoming more challenging.

Division II is mostly partial scholarships, while Division III is academic-based scholarships. NAIA is a different division entirely and has partial and some full scholarships. Each coach needs to plan what he/she has available in scholarship funding over the four years, so you will know what you can offer a recruit compared to your competition and stay within the NCAA limits. If you are a Division I school, then it is about making sure you have balance in your scholarship recruiting over four years to keep your program consistently strong.

Equivalency Sport Scholarship
Offering Advice

Equivalency sport scholarship allocation is not easy to balance. I have developed a strategy system that works for coaches based on a recruiting incident from the early 1990s.

There was a great college athlete in an equivalency sport who eventually won two Olympic gold medals. What happened in the equivalency scholarship recruitment of this athlete was very instrumental in how I provide recommendations to coaches today.

The recruit was in the top five nationally and UCLA was ahead. He wanted a full scholarship to go to college, but our coach thought that a 90% scholarship was fair because he needed a little development to be an immediate Olympian.

I tried reasoning with the coach that if he spent so much time recruiting the future Olympian, including out-of-state home and official visits, plus evaluations, why wouldn't he provide the last 10% to close the deal (roughly $2000 in scholarship funds at the time)?

The coach believed in what he was doing, which I understood. However, I felt then and still feel today it is more important to have the recruit in your program as an impact athlete over splitting the scholarship funds for two or three depth recruits. The recruit went elsewhere and had a great college career. We replaced him with two depth recruits that did not have an impact. I can't rule out that not offering the full scholarship cost us an NCAA title.

For a coach to provide slightly more scholarship in his four-year plan by giving an impact recruit up to 10% more scholarship makes more sense than having him compete against you for four years. Also once you lose him/her, then you are getting a prospect or prospects usually not as strong even at less scholarship money. Depth is nice, but star athletes are the ones who still usually win events and titles for your program.

The equivalency recruiting advice rule that was utilized from that point forward was: If a coach spends his/her most time on an impact No. 1 type recruit, then he/she should be willing to provide slightly more scholarship funds than he/she wants to do. This would be approximately 10% over the total amount that the coach was planning to offer on a major scholarship (a half scholarship or less would be up to 5% more for example), provided the coach can immediately close the commitment. It is better to have the recruit compete for you, than against your team in almost every case if the coach's evaluation is accurate.

Parents need to be realistic in the value they think their son or daughter is worth in an equivalency sport. However, the coach has to project out the immediate program value of that recruit over the first two college years in being willing to increase a final offer.

Parents/Recruits: If you are being recruited in a head count sport, you are looking for a full scholarship that can now include the "Cost of Attendance" so you have no family out-of-pocket expenses.

Some colleges outside of the top five major conferences may not have the budget to include the "Cost of Attendance" provision with the full scholarship. Some smaller schools in Division I may not have the NCAA limit of full scholarships in each sport (see chart), so they may offer you less than a full to meet their financial budgets. You have to consider these options in considering that school. Almost all Division I schools are fully funded in each head count sport with everything covered with a full scholarship.

For equivalency sports, it can be very much of a negotiation battle for how much scholarship you will be offered since there are limited full scholarships in putting together a balanced team. If you are the best in that Olympic sport, then you will be offered a major scholarship. However, in a lot of cases, recruits and parents have to weigh a smaller offer at a more powerful overall college vs. a bigger offer at a college that may not have as many academic or athletic resources.

It is not an easy decision because college is so expensive and you want to avoid taking out college loans if possible. Division II is a viable alternative as most schools have athletic scholarship funding (see chart below). It may be better for your son or daughter to compete right away and be happier in a smaller environment. Academic and financial aid may also be possible.

Scholarship offering is where asking questions of the head coach becomes most important. At the start of the senior year, you can ask for the scholarship offer to be put into writing. Some schools start small and then promise increases each year. You can ask to see that in writing from the head coach so you have paperwork. You can't always trust verbal offers in equivalency sports since college costs change and coaches can change.

Doing your homework is so important in checking and comparing schools and offers. Get the scholarship offer in writing in advance of the letter of intent being mailed to you so you know what is being offered. It gives you time to discuss any discrepancies in what you believe you were promised before signing.

My advice is to use the "College Comparison Chart" (end of chapter 6). Think of college as a long-range life-changing business decision. Scholarship offers are definitely important, but taking less at the school with more long-term career, academic and athletic resources many times is better for your future. The old saying of being "a big fish in a small pond" vs. being "a small fish in a big pond"[4] is very true for Olympic sport equivalency recruiting.

It is so important to do your homework before deciding. It makes for the best college future and a positive long range decision. The "NCAA Guide for College-Bound Student-Athletes"[5] is an excellent resource and every college should have that available for you as a permissible recruiting item. The number of scholarships available and whether it is a "head count" or "equivalency" sport is listed below.

COLLEGE MEN'S SPORTS SCHOLARSHIP LIMITS[6]

SPORT	NCAA I	NCAA II
Baseball (Equivalency)	11.7	9
Basketball (Head Count)	13	10
Cross Country/Track (Equivalency)	12.6	12.6
Fencing (Equivalency)	4.5	4.5
Football (FBS Head Count)	85	36
Football (1AA, FCS)	63	–
Golf (Equivalency)	4.5	3.6
Gymnastics (Equivalency)	6.3	5.4

---

4 http://www.phrases.org.uk/meanings/big-fish-in-a-small-pond.html

5 NCAA.org website

6 NCAA.org website

Ice Hockey (Equivalency)	18	13.5
Lacrosse (Equivalency)	12.6	10.8
Rifle (Equivalency-women also)	3.6	3.6
Soccer (Equivalency)	9.9	9
Swimming & Diving (Equivalency)	9.9	8.1
Tennis (Equivalency)	4.5	4.5
Volleyball (Equivalency)	4.5	4.5
Water Polo (Equivalency)	4.5	4.5
Wrestling (Equivalency)	9.9	9

COLLEGE WOMEN'S SPORTS SCHOLARSHIP LIMITS[7]

SPORT	NCAA I	NCAA II
Basketball (Head Count)	15	10
Bowling (Equivalency)	5	5
Cross Country/Track (Equivalency)	18	12.6
Equestrian (Equivalency)	15	15
Fencing (Equivalency)	5	4.5
Field Hockey (Equivalency)	12	6.3
Golf (Equivalency)	6	5.4
Gymnastics (Head Count)	12	6
Ice Hockey (Equivalency)	18	18
Lacrosse (Equivalency)	12	9.9
Rifle (Equivalency-coed with men)	3.6	3.6
Rowing (Equivalency)	20	20
Rugby (Equivalency)	12	12
Sand Volleyball (Equivalency)	6	5
Soccer (Equivalency)	14	9.9
Softball (Equivalency)	12	7.2
Swimming & Diving (Equivalency)	14	8.1
Tennis (Head Count)	8	6
Volleyball (Head Count)	12	8
Water Polo (Equivalency)	8	8

7 NCAA.org website

Financial Aid: Coaches/Parents/Recruits: Applying and receiving financial aid/government & state grants/academic scholarships/low interest loans can benefit coaches, parents and recruits so that a recruit can afford to attend the college he/she really wants.

This can work for head count sports where a recruit can qualify for up to a full scholarship in financial aid and Pell Grants (federal need based grants for low income students that do not have to be repaid)[8]. This can then open another athletic scholarship to build a stronger team. Financial aid need is much more likely in the equivalency sports where there are few full scholarships to pay for the costs of college.

Parents should always apply for financial aid and low interest loans even if they believe they won't qualify. More people qualify for some type of aid compared to what the average parent thinks, because there are so many factors involved.

Universities and states have their own types of financial aid, grants and academic scholarships that can reduce the cost of an education to go with government-based aid. Most athletic departments also have a "special needs" fund for student-athletes who qualify for financial aid for necessary college costs. You have to apply for financial aid to find out where you stand.

It is tough to be in a family where your son/daughter may owe $25,000 to $35,000 (average amount for non-full scholarship student-athletes) in loans after college. However, by applying you can see what is possible in your efforts to cover what it costs to attend a top college. If you are from a low-income family, your son or daughter can keep Pell Grant money up to the listed college cost of attendance at the school. This is provided everything isn't covered in the athletic scholarship.

There is little difference in the overall total cost percentage covered in the basic financial aid packages from public to private colleges. There may be a slight difference from individual schools in their policies and their own school aid packages. However, overall the government financial aid packages are similar in the percentage paid of the total cost of a school as well as the money available from a Pell Grant subsidy.

---

8 Pellgrants.educationconnection.com website

Don't let a private school tell you its financial package is better than the public school because it is worth more money. The key is looking at the percentage of the total college costs that are covered in determining if it is really better.

The website for applying for financial aid is www.fafsa.ed.gov[9] and it can benefit a family or school only when you see what you may qualify for in aid and loans. Most United States applying deadlines are at the start of March of the senior year of high school and the application is traditionally available at the start of January. There is a sample estimator program on the FAFSA website where you can see what you may qualify for in aid in advance.

---

9 WWW.fafsa.ed.gov website

CHAPTER 5

NCAA Admissions/Eligibility
for Your Advantage

All colleges, regardless of division or reputation, have some type of athletic admissions system. That means that a top athletic recruit, regardless of sport, may not need the same academic profile in terms of grades, advanced classes and test scores as a regular student applying to that university to be admitted. There may be basic college academic minimums, but each case for a top athletic recruit is taken on its own merits.

This chapter provides a better understanding of how the athletic admissions system can be utilized to benefit coaches in recruiting. It will also show how scholarship options are less for your son/daughter if he/she isn't on top of the required academics.

Coaches: Athletic Admissions to your university is one of the most overlooked advantages that coaches have in the recruiting process if used properly. It can be as big an advantage for recruiting the 4.0 straight "A" student as well as the 2.3 student that is just hoping to make NCAA eligibility to be able to play under the new recruiting rules going into effect in fall of 2016.

Every college utilizes some form of Athletic Admissions whether a great academic or athletic school. Some schools have a general admissions office or officer that reviews student-athlete admissions. Others have an athletic admissions committee or key faculty person that reviews athletic admissions. I know colleges that have turned down 4.0 students because a 3.3 was a better athletic fit and I know schools that have admitted 2.3 students and turned down a 3.5 student in the same sport for athletic reasons.

Some colleges require a recruit to turn in the college application and essays to be early admitted before regular students. Others now do early admissions off a high school transcript as soon as 11th grade. Then as a coach you can have the recruit bypass the required essays and simply turn in the standard college application with the required fee. Schools from the same academic system or conference can be completely different in their admissions/recruiting approach. You need to turn your admissions system into an advantage.

Student-athletes get quizzed all the time on what they did on their official or unofficial visits. However, they are seldom asked what they did in the admissions process or when they were told they were pre-admitted to a university. Knowing how your rivals operate can help you make comparisons with how your university handle things. The edge could be in gaining early commitments.

If you are an academic university with higher admission standards than your competition, then telling a student-athlete and parents that you really want as early a commitment as possible after you have done pre-admissions can be a decided advantage. It also gives you a chance to provide a deadline to make a decision on a scholarship. This is especially true if your competition may struggle to admit the same student-athlete early or doesn't have an admission system as strong as yours for student-athletes to be pre-admitted.

Very few coaches know how their opponents operate from an academic standpoint, but always want to know everything athletically. Academic knowledge can be to your advantage, so be aware of where it can help you so you don't lose out in this category. This becomes especially relevant with scholarships being offered earlier and earlier.

Four Keys to Successfully Utilizing Admissions/Eligibility

1. Ask for transcripts early—no later than the second semester of 10th grade on an impact five-star athlete who you know everyone

wants and after 10th grade on anyone else you have a scholarship interest in or have offered. Make sure you know what classes the recruit needs to take and what grades are needed in 11th and 12th grade to be admitted to your school **(ask recruit to join NCAA Eligibility Center before the start of 11th grade).**

2. Have any recruits you want take the SAT/ACT as early as possible. This is essential in seeing if anything additionally needs to be done for your admissions.   Try to get the test taken for the first time in June of the sophomore year (both SAT/ACT are offered). If later, have the PSAT/PACT taken in the fall of 11th grade (most high schools do it then) and the regular test as soon as possible afterwards.

    The key to your recruiting is not waiting for an SAT/ACT test to be taken until the senior year of high school. This is especially true when you have tougher admission standards. You need to know as much in advance about the admissibility of the recruit and how he/she fits into your four-year scholarship plan. You don't want to waste time and effort waiting for a top recruit who may or may not qualify for your program when you can get someone else of similar quality without the academic issues.

3. If it comes down to two recruits for one scholarship, I recommend taking the better student. The reason is simple. That person projects to be better prepared academically, which usually provides for a better overall college experience. This puts less strain on you and your academic staff for the recruit to remain eligible to compete.

    Coaches are not always academic miracle workers. I have seen coaching failures in believing that a recruit, who has struggled throughout high school and has a lower SAT/ACT, will be as successful athletically as they would have been by attending a less demanding academic college.   The academic pressure to remain eligible can cause athletic problems and each year becomes more stressful as a recruit moves into his/ her major.

4. Don't delay the official visit to the end of the senior year recruiting period if you think a recruit may commit to another school if they admit him/her. The recruit may like the other school as much or better and a guaranteed scholarship offer can be the difference in having your visit canceled.

From experience, I believe that having the first or second official visit has become more beneficial than the fourth or fifth. This is especially an advantage if you have the chance to get the final visits canceled through using your early admissions process. Use your academics to set a deadline for the recruit if he/she is the only student you can have admitted with that profile. If you don't get the reaction you want, move onto the next recruit on your list.

Setting a deadline for making a commitment almost always lets you know where you stand in the recruiting process. Recruits don't want to miss out on the scholarship they want if it is your college.

Possible Perks for Early Commitment to Your School

1. Pre-priority athletic admissions—bypass university application essays
2. Guaranteed priority housing, roommate selection, best campus location
3. 4 or 5-year guaranteed scholarship at level of commitment; start out ahead
4. Priority parking if have car for college; this can be important
5. Paying for pre-season housing/holiday training expenses to max of NCAA rule allowance
6. Priority/individual tutoring year-round; individual is big plus
7. Paying for 100% of summer school prior to start of college
8. Guaranteed Summer Job around Summer School/Winter Job if on-campus

9. Spring vacation stipend/housing if needed to stay on-campus to train

10. Recommendations or admission priority for your graduate schools

Parents/Recruits: You should try in the recruiting process to ask a series of key questions based on how strong an academic student your son/daughter is in high school. Here are some examples of questions that you could ask of the head coach/recruiting coach to make sure that admissions is moving forward for your teenager.

1. Based on the HS transcript, has my son/daughter been pre-admitted to your university?
2. What SAT/ACT score does he/she need to be admitted with the grades?
3. Based on reviewing his/her grades and test results, what else is needed to be admitted?
4. If I am admitted to your school, do I have a scholarship?
5. When will you know when I am admitted to your school? Has another recruit been admitted? If yes, what was his/her academic profile?

Don't be afraid to put some pressure on the head coach as admissions can work both ways in helping you make the right college decision. A lot of schools say one thing to one recruit and change it with another recruit depending upon how important the recruit is as a scholarship student-athlete. Make sure you understand the process and know the time frames for athletic admission. Coaches usually know early on their top recruits if they are pre-admitted, so ask the questions and compare. Get something in writing if you can.
Check with other parents of current student-athletes as to when their son/daughter was admitted and were there any restrictions or test requirements put on the admission. This way you know what is needed from your top schools. All schools have some type of athletic admissions. There is always a system of timing when they know if a top recruit is pre-admitted or not.

If you aren't a top recruit, the coach will still know when you will be admitted within their process and ask for a time frame. Remember the best student doesn't always get admitted through athletic admissions, but having better grades and test scores allows a family to put pressure for an answer on the head coach.

Application—Find out if the college application is really needed in advance of the general student for the admissions process if your top school already has your transcripts. Sometimes it is a coach's way of stalling you in the process so he/she can see if it can get the first recruit to commit while you wait.

The same goes with the college essay process. This is usually another stalling method of academic colleges and the essay isn't really needed if you are admitted through athletic admissions. Again checking with other parents and recruits is your best source. You want to know whether you are getting accurate information. You need to know whether you are a priority for the university or down the list whom they want to stall until the top recruit makes his/her decision.

The NCAA Eligibility Center[10] is very important in recruiting. A potential college student-athlete should register by no later than the start of llth grade. The reason is to make sure he/she is taking the right classes necessary for college eligibility. Your high school will send the official transcript through ninth and tenth grade for NCAA evaluation. You will then be able to see how you are progressing in meeting both the necessary number of classes and required GPA. It is your responsibility to know what classes and test score you need to be eligible to compete in college.

2016 NCAA Eligibility Grade-Point-Average (taken from the "NCAA Guide for College-Bound Student-Athletes"[11])

Incoming college student-athletes must present a grade-point average that predicts academic success at the collegiate level.

---

10 http://web1.ncaa.org/ECWR2/NCAA_EMS/NCAA.jsp
11 NCAA.org website

- Beginning August 1, 2016, a recruit must earn at least a 2.300 GPA in NCAA core courses to be eligible to compete in the first year of college.
- To receive an athletic scholarship and practice, a recruit must earn at least a 2.000 GPA in required NCAA core courses.
- Only courses that appear on the high school's list of NCAA courses will be used to calculate your GPA for NCAA eligibility purposes. For a complete list of your school's courses, visit www. eligibilitycenter.org
- Once 10 core courses are "locked in" prior to the start of your seventh high school semester (usually the start of 12th grade), you can't take those classes over again to improve your GPA.
- Division I uses a sliding scale to match test scores and core GPAs. You have to reach the bottom limits to compete in your first year of college.

NCAA Division I Sliding Scale for Eligibility

Use for Division I beginning August 1, 2016

Core GPA	SAT	ACT
3.550 & above	400	37
3.525	410	38
3.500	420	39
3.475	430	40
3.450	440	41
3.425	450	41
3.400	460	42
3.375	470	42
3.350	480	43
3.325	490	44
3.300	500	44
3.275	510	45
3.250	520	46
3.225	530	46

* NCAA.org website

Core GPA	SAT	ACT
3.200	540	47
3.175	550	47
3.150	560	48
3.125	570	49
3.100	580	49
3.075	590	50
3.050	600	50
3.025	610	51
3.000	620	52
2.975	630	52
2.950	640	53
2.925	650	53
2.900	660	54
2.875	670	55
2.850	680	56
2.825	690	56
2.800	700	57
2.775	710	58
2.750	720	59
2.725	730	60
2.700	740	61
2.675	750	61
2.650	760	62
2.625	770	63
2.600	780	64
2.575	790	65
2.550	800	66
2.525	810	67
2.500	800	68
2.475	830	69
2.450	840	70
2.425	850	70
2.400	860	71
2.375	870	72
2.350	880	73
2.325	890	74
2.300	900	75
2.275	910	76
2.250	920	77
2.225	930	78
2.200	940	79
2.175	950	80
2.150	960	81
2.125	970	82
2.100	980	83

Important Eligibility Phone Numbers/Websites
NCAA: (317) 917-6222 www.NCAA.org
NCAA ELIGIBILITY: (877)-262-1492 www.web1.NCAA.org
SAT: (866)-756-7346 www.sat.Collegeboard.org
ACT: (319)-337-1270 www.actstudent.org

Having NBA stars at your home events can help with your "Circle of Influence" or "Team" approach to recruiting

CHAPTER 6

"Circle of Influence" Works in Recruiting

C oaches: There is so much more that goes into the recruiting process than finding a recruit that can fill the spot you need in your program. Many coaches forget about the people around the recruit and spend too much time working on just the personal relationship with the recruit to cultivate him or her to go to their university. The "Circle of Influence" is based on dividing a circle into eight parts and utilizing all eight parts in the recruiting process to get the final decision to go your way.

If you face "distrust" during the recruiting process about your program, my advice is deal with the "distrust" right away. Make sure you have solved the problem or consider moving onto the next recruit. One or two "distrusts" can be enough to cost you the recruit coming to your school. The advice is to cut your losses as soon as the "distrust" become too much of a problem to overcome vs. your competition, which may have a better match. The "Circle of Influence" system works well in determining your match with the recruit, his family and other associates.

"Circle of Influence" Breakdown: It is important for a coaching staff to have touched all aspects of the "Circle of Influence" in recruiting. This way there are no surprises at decision time if the recruit picks your competition. The "Circle of Influence" is labeled as 1) Parents 2) Children/ Close Friends 3) Club & HS Coach, Private Coach 4) Favorite Teacher/ Class/Counselor 5) Religious Leader/Family Advisor 6) Media-Local Prep Writer, Radio/TV Person around team 7) Social Media-Contacts on Facebook, Twitter posts, Instagram, YouTube, New Media 8) Your

Matchup in Academics, Social Life, School Location, Facilities, Campus Resources vs. Competition.

Tracking those eight areas allow for a positive impression of your program and your university. This provides you the best chances of consistent recruiting success.

For 1) and 2) it is important to keep the parents informed in the recruiting process through emails, letters, materials and phone calls at least once a month as permitted by NCAA rules as you approach the decision. Many parents today want to be very active with their sons or daughters throughout the entire recruiting. They are a great source of information about your competition and what is most important in making the final decision for your college. Finding out where brothers and sisters went to college or how involved/how close they are to the recruit (if younger) plays a role.

Close friends and where they are going to school or want to go to school also play a role. From my experiences, boyfriends of female recruits are more influential in the majority of cases, than the girlfriends influencing male recruits. Males tend to do what they want or their parents want (in many cases parents want a fresh start away from the relationship), while females tend to put more weight into where the boyfriends want them to go.

For 3) and 4) you need to find out if the club coach (usually more important than the high school one) is injecting himself or herself into the recruiting process. They can be very helpful or very hurtful pending on wanting their feelings heard. Be aware there could be another outside factor involved such as a shoe company (primarily in basketball or track & field) or a self-appointed agent (usually football/baseball) looking at the recruit's future as his or her future "meal ticket." Finding out what the coach knows and thinks pays dividends in trying to close the deal.

Some high school counselors, especially at private academic schools or with a great academic student, like to be part of the process. They tend to go against you if you work for a public college over a private college, because they usually believe the private education is better.

It is important to meet with the counselor or send them materials about your program and academic services so they can be turned into a positive and not a negative. The same also holds true for a borderline NCAA qualifier where you need the counselor to help you put the recruit into the right academic classes to meet the new NCAA eligibility standards. If a recruit has a preferred major, it is possible it is because of a favorite teacher or class taken at the high school. It is worth your time to find out this valuable information.

For 5), 6) and 7) it becomes significant if these factors are a major part of the final decision making process. If religion is a factor or important to your university, then you want to make it a part of the official or unofficial visit. If you have your own Athletes-In-Action or Bible Study chapters tied to the athletic department, make sure you show this to the recruit and parents if it is going to be a decision maker.

Contacting the local high school sportswriters/your college recruiting website writers or the specialized sport people involved in covering the recruit's games/matches/meets/competitions usually can provide valuable information. They know if the recruit has shown any indication of a favorite school if a scholarship is offered or what schools have shown the most interest.

These individuals want to be in the loop on a top recruit to get the story for their website or Twitter account. They try to stay involved so you can work with them along the way in helping you gain valuable insights.

Social media is the newest influential factor in recruiting. It has become more and more important as the 2010s advanced. First it was Facebook, but now Twitter seems to be the most important outlet with the top recruits. However, don't rule out looking at other aspects of social media such as Instagram, YouTube or Vine or something new that is coming out.

You need to monitor the recruit on social media the best you can under the NCAA rules (it is a stretch of NCAA rules, but your athletes may be able to help you if they have a relationship with the recruit). You want to look for pictures on Facebook when they have visited other schools and Twitter posts as to clues as to how you are doing in the recruiting process. You should be able to figure out pretty easily where you stand with the recruit if you follow the message tree.

A recruit-tracking service I like is "Preptracker," which provides even more daily details than Google alerts, for example. The more you can read or review daily, the better the ability to land the recruit. More importantly, if you are doing the job in the recruiting process, you should see positive messages about your program on the same sites. You can never have too much recruiting information. Tracking the recruit you want should begin as early as ninth or tenth grade.

The recruiting intangibles revolve around pie piece eight. The "ABC-123" Recruiting Matchup System (see chapter 8) has been developed to help analyze your chances of being successful based on your school needs vs. what the recruit is looking for. You need to ask the right questions in the first phone call or first meeting. Use biography sheets to your advantage to learn as much as you can about your recruits and the other individuals tied to the "Circle of Influence."

Make sure that the "Circle of Influence" knows how your university stacks up in key areas of the decision-making process. This includes areas such as coaching, academics, facilities, housing, social benefits, area for living and other factors that you utilize in showcasing your school resources.

Parents/Recruits: Gathering as much information as possible to make the correct college decision is vital in the process. My advice is to ask for college opinions from individuals you trust that can be outside of your immediate family or your main club or high school coach.

Utilize your friendships with other club/league coaches, former teammates or other athletes who have gone to that college or been through the recruiting experience. Parents/recruits should also talk to other parents, teachers and your counselor. It doesn't hurt to talk to friends making similar college decisions and others you may be regularly in touch with to get their views.

You don't want to make a quick or rushed decision the first time you visit a college or with the first offer you receive without making sure it meets your essentials. The top athletic college to offer you a scholarship is not necessarily the best one for your future.

My advice is to put together a list of what things are important in selecting your college. Divide it academically, athletically and socially/intangibles to make the final decision. In this chapter is the "College Comparison Chart" that has been developed specifically to help make that necessary decision among your top three college choices (you should be able to realistically narrow it down).

COLLEGE COMPARISON CHART BY CATEGORY— RATE 1 BEST, 2 SECOND, 3 THIRD

CATEGORY	SCHOOL	#1	#2	#3

ACADEMICS:
Prestige of Degree
Alumni Networking
Graduate on Time
Major of Interest
Individual Tutoring
Pre-Enrollment Classes
Quarter vs. Semester
Paid Summer School
Summer Internship
Grad School Chance
Finish Degree in 5th year
Athletic Academic Success Rate

ATHLETICS:
Scholarship Money
Guaranteed 4 or 5 Years
Team Success
Coaches Success
Athlete Success Rate
School Overall Success
Post-College Athletic Success
Facilities in Your Sport
Overall Campus Facilities
Dorm for Athletes

Off-Campus Living
Weight Room
Training Room
Sports Medicine
Training Table/Food

SOCIAL/INTANGIBLES
Feel Most Comfortable
Happiness of Other Athletes
Immediate Playing Time
Stability of Head Coach
Campus Location
Recreation Activities
Local Entertainment/Fun
Parents See Me Compete
Siblings, Friends, Relatives
Can Go Pro/Get Job I Want
Media Exposure
School Website/Media
Pride in Going There
Rank Scores by Most "Bests" in the Categories:

CHAPTER 7

"TEAM" Recruiting Approach

The "TEAM" (Togetherness, Excellence, Achievement, Momentum) recruiting approach is designed to maximize the college's ability to land top recruits by producing the most effective campus official and unofficial visits. It also helps parents and recruits know what the college best showcases in terms of its athletic and academic resources.

Coaches: "TEAM" is a recruiting approach that works the best for you to be able to close your recruits through providing the best overall quality experience for parents and recruits on both the unofficial and official campus visits.

"TEAM" has brought recruiting success after success by having each sport utilizing the same message in "selling" its school. This includes key staff members assisting by utilizing the same philosophy when interacting with recruits, parents and current student-athletes.

Football/basketball should have the same fundamental recruiting message as soccer, which should have the same basic message as volleyball. This message, theme, philosophy, motto, slogan should be set through the Athletic Director. It needs to be followed by the various sport coaches and staffs when they meet with recruits along with current and former student-athletes/parents. It should also involve their booster groups supporting the same athletic message.

An example would be that all sports would use the same short message, theme or slogan in correspondence or when speaking to current student-athletes, recruits or boosters. That phrase would be connected every time it is heard publicly to that college as the branding message.

Consistency is so important in acceptance of that phrase being connected directly to your school.

T—The "T" stands for the "togetherness" an athletic department needs to have among its staff, coaches and student-athletes in the recruiting process. Having regular activities where you can bring your department together for a common goal is vital. Begin the start of the academic school year with an event for all student-athletes, coaches and staff (August/September depending upon whether you are a semester/ quarter school) initiates the "togetherness." Your athletic director can publicize the message again at that time so it makes a lasting impression.

Then close the academic year with an exciting senior class athletic graduation activity to unite your overall program going into summer. This is a day when virtually everyone is happy and pictures for the athletic website are a must.

Having special events such as "Junior Days" at a variety of athletic dates where you can intermix recruits with your current student-athletes works very well. The coaches should sit with parents of recruits around their student-athletes, while they sit with the recruits. This helps in the "togetherness" approach.

Staff and coaches should have their own quarterly events to share information. This can help bond a program to work together for the same common recruiting goals. There needs to be solid support among the coaches. The football and basketball programs must also participate by encouraging their teams to attend other sports events, along with meeting other sport top recruits on visits.

E—The "E" stands for "excellence." You want "excellence" in everything you do in your program with regard to recruiting. This goes from the correspondence you send to recruits to the materials available when visiting the campus to your sport website to the commitment stage through unofficial and official visits and then finishing through the time the recruit enrolls at your university. Some coaches forget about the recruit after signing day, which is a mistake in starting the "team" approach early. Your new signees can be your best future recruiters.

Each coaching staff should have regular weekly recruiting meetings (30 to 60 minutes) to be on the same page. You want to make sure the other staff units that work with your program also strive for the "excellence" you need. The head coach should have a four-year scholarship plan where the staff is working together to maximize the "team" performance. Recruits have to know that "excellence" is what you are striving for on and off the playing surface and you want them to be a part of something special in your program.

A—The "A" stands for "achievement." You want high "achievement" for the overall athletic program and especially your own sport in and out of the classroom. You want recruits and their parents to know everything your university/athletic department does well. Recruits should know this from your athletic website, your own sport website and college website (it is critical to have an athletic link on the university front page for easy access). Use whatever other social media is available to promote and market your program and the overall university accomplishments.

You need consistent "achievement" to attract the best recruits and give them and their parents the excitement that they are becoming part of something special at your college. Many coaches rely just on accomplishments in their sport when they should be including not only other sports, but highlights of your university and alumni.

Recruits are media savvy and love links to videos that help your recruiting cause. Parents should be included and mail is a good way to do it. Make sure they have your Twitter account address and if you have a school YouTube site to follow.

M—The "M" stands for "momentum." You utilize "togetherness" to develop "excellence" and "achievement" and this brings "momentum" to your university, athletic department and to your program. "Momentum" is so important and necessary to capture the attention of your potential recruits and parents.

Then use the "momentum" at its highest point to commit the recruits you want in the process. All four categories work together to bring the "TEAM" concept to life and it does work well for all college sports. It is so important to have your athletic department working together for a common message. The "TEAM" approach is something you need to win consistently and it works.

Four Ways the "TEAM" Approach can Improve your Recruiting

A. The athletic department coaches should have quarterly group meetings (August before official visits start; December after fall signing period as football visits get going; Mid-March prior to the NCAA Basketball Tournament and before April letters of intent; May-June right after the school year is completed).

These meetings are to discuss as a coaching group what works and doesn't work in recruiting for the university. One sport can always learn something from another sport that is successful. Develop a working plan for which restaurants, hotels, campus hangouts, transportation, etc. works best for recruiting. The key is having the various sports on the same page using the same tools so that the same message is promoted sport by sport.

Budgets may be different by sport, but the "TEAM" approach can be the same in concept. Both the December and June meetings should be debriefing campus visit activities and planning for "Junior Days," summer evaluations and camps and improving unofficial visits.

B. It is essential to involve the administration and staff in the recruiting process. Areas of involvement should include the athletic director, sport coordinators, academic coordinator and staff, weight room staff, athletic training room personnel and a combination of sports publicity, marketing and fundraising members.

These individuals need to be part of your "TEAM" approach and you need to develop their roles for official and unofficial visits. The more staff participation, the better, as long as they know their roles. You need to review in advance what they are going to say to your recruits. Practice makes perfect in working with staff. Establish "talking points" with each unit that best works with your recruiting message.

C. Decide what other aspects of campus life and which personnel should be included in your "TEAM" approach. What I recommend is utilizing the University President/Chancellor for impact/5 star recruits in all sports (not just football or men's basketball). If you can utilize that important person for your top sport recruit who could be the next All-American, then it is a positive to let the recruit know he/she was important enough that the head of the university wanted to meet. Be very selective and the involvement means that much more.

Develop a group of selected professors in the most significant or important academic departments in your college. The Nobel Prize/department award winner may not be the best recruiter. You want someone in the department who can talk about the Nobel Prize winner or top professor that will have the best effect on you landing the recruit. The most likely departments where you need recruiting help are Business, Communications, Sports Medicine, Education and Engineering.

If you have football at your university it is great to invite these individuals and their spouses and families to your pre-game football picnics (see official/unofficial visit section). If you are doing on-campus "Junior Days," have the professors invited to attend the meal/event to meet your top recruits. If you can do the campus meal, it is great if there is a private dining room in the dorms where you can have current student-athletes eat the meal with the recruits. Because it is on campus, it gives you more flexibility with NCAA rules to involve your student-athletes as a vital part of the "TEAM" process.

D. One of the most overlooked aspects of recruiting is the pre-recruit meeting with your team and the post-visit debriefing. Your student-athletes need to buy into the recruiting message as part of the "TEAM" approach. You need to talk to your host(s) immediately after the visit for their impressions of the visit, both good and bad as well as other staff involved.

You should compare notes with other coaches about their visits especially if you did some of the same activities such as using the same hotel (how was check-in?), same restaurant (did you feel you were treated like a VIP?), went to an athletic event (how was entry, seats, atmosphere?). The more information you have, the better for future recruiting.

Parents/Recruits: You want to attend a university where athletics is important and your sport is appreciated by its fellow student-athletes. There are significant things to review in deciding upon a college. When you make a campus visit, there are telltale signs of where you and your sport fit in and how well those team members interact with the other sport student-athletes.

A. Don't be afraid ask the tough questions. What is the goal of the coach in your sport and how does it fit into the mission of the athletic department and the university? How does your son or daughter fit into the team? What role does the coach expect him/her to play? How long does the head coach expect to stay there (contract length, winning-losing, advancing to a higher level, going pro, etc.)? How were you treated by the school compared to other schools you have visited? Did the campus visit meet your expectations? Is there a "TEAM" concept?

B. The more people you meet, the more likely you are a realistic recruit for that program and they could have a spot for you. This includes meeting with academics, facilities, department administrators, faculty, student-athletes, etc. Try to meet or talk to someone you know in another sport in the program and compare resources. The best programs have the same resources for all sports and the athletes feel very united as a group. Are the athletes happy there?

C. The most important question to ask at the end of the visit is, "Can I see myself going to this university and being happy here athletically, academically and socially?" If the answer is yes, then you should follow with a thank-you note or email to show your appreciation. It isn't done that often and makes a positive impression on the coaching staff. A recruit can commit anytime he/she if offered the scholarship.

It doesn't matter how strong your overall program is nationally, you can still land top recruits by utilizing the "TEAM" system. It makes working at that program so much better when the department is united. You will see the success in all aspects of the college experience. It will impress parents/recruits and they will want to be a part of something special.

10 Unique Ideas to Try in "TEAM" Recruiting Approach

I want coaches to utilize unique and memorable recruiting ideas that would separate them from the competition. This could be for official or unofficial visits or off-campus contacts. The ideas should be discussed with other coaches, so they could use them as part of the "TEAM" approach to recruiting. It is important to have the football and basketball coaches believe in the system because they could provide valuable support roles in helping the other coaches by meeting their top recruits on campus visits or seeing them at their home events.

Here are 10 actual recruiting stories that can stimulate coaches from one sport to do something with another coach/sport for a recruiting advantage. For parents/recruits, this may provide some insights to see if a college does something memorable in your recruiting activities.

1. A head coach used an off-campus contact (instead of the traditional home visit) to attend a "Harry Potter" movie with a top recruit because she was totally into the book series. The coach then showed her information about the school's "Quidditch" club team. This extra step was a positive in her coming to our college.

2. A coach found that food was a major recruiting issue with his top recruit. The athlete loved Asian food and after asking other coaches, I found him the best Chinese/Japanese buffet on the Westside to go to for the official visit dinner. He also loved the

food in the dorms (part of the official visit) and the wide variety of local restaurants. The food was a definite factor in him coming to school and he became an All-American.

3. We used the knowledge about a water sport recruit that was totally into college basketball. The coach brought the recruit and his father into the UCLA basketball locker room after the game and they got to meet the head coach and some team members. That exciting memory was likely a factor in his deciding to attend here over the other local college option.

4. A female recruit's dad was a college football player. We made sure we got him into the football locker room after a game to meet the head coach and team members. This helped win him over for she signed with us.

5. The parents of a top recruit loved our athletic tradition, so we had them meet renowned basketball Coach John Wooden on the visit. Another set of parents admired Olympic Decathlon gold medalist Rafer Johnson when they were growing up and we made sure they met at a pre-game football picnic. Both legends put a positive spin on our university and made the parents believe in the school's tradition. Both recruits signed a letter of intent with us.

6. We tried something different for an official visit for a top football recruit. The football coaches agreed to let him attend a home women's volleyball match on a Friday night instead of being at the hotel with the football team before the next-day game because his sister played club volleyball and he loved the sport. We then had other current student-athletes from different sports recruit him at the event. It worked out well and he signed with us.

7. Our coaches received NCAA approval on an unofficial visit for a top two-sport recruit to go out to sea on the marine biology boat at the off-campus academic facility. We got approval because it was her academic interest. She said it was her best unofficial visit, but she still went to a rival college in the end.

8. We alerted the college football and basketball coaches to say hello to other sport high school coaches during a recruiting school visit when they were evaluating other top athletes at the same

place. Then we followed by having the same coach or even head coach say hello or meet in person with the scholarship recruit and family on a campus visit ("TEAM" concept in action). It made a difference in the recruiting visits of a few Olympic sport athletes from out-of-state high schools that the football and basketball coaches cared about the other sports.

9. When there was a recruiting official-visit bus trip to an off-campus athletic event facility, we had multiple teams go together on the same bus to enhance the recruiting experience (it also saved on budget). It was a major advantage to have two sports interacting together and then show team highlight videos on the bus. This allowed time for coaches to sit and talk to parents. Recruits usually committed because they enjoyed this type of "TEAM" interaction.

10. We drove a recruit interested in a television broadcast career to a taping of a cable sports show on the official visit. We then had her talk to the announcers about a career in media. Doing something extra in one sport was so successful that it worked again for another sport with a media-interested recruit. Look for innovative ideas on the campus visits to fulfill recruits' academic interests to go with showcasing the sport.

Even if you appear to be leading for a recruit, never take anything for granted in the recruiting process or you may end up disappointed at the end. Using the "TEAM" system works for any college athletic program.

CHAPTER 8

"ABC-123" Recruiting Matchup System

The "ABC-123" Recruiting Matchup System can work for all sports as you try to build your program nationally. This is a specialized recruiting system that works best if coaches are realistic in their approach to evaluating recruits on athletic ability combined with the overall match with their colleges. It is especially designed for the mid-major and other programs that want to improve their national success rate. It also helps other programs that are looking to move up in their conference standings by having better local success or trying to maximize recruiting budgets by reducing recruiting mistakes.

Athletic Ability vs. Overall Matchup with your University

AA	**BA**	**CA**
AB	**BB**	**CB**
AC	**BC**	**CC**
AD		
AF		
	OR	
11	21	31
12	22	32
13	23	33
14		
15		

Most college recruiting evaluation systems involve rating recruits from 1 to 5 stars or an A to F system based on athletic ability. What the "ABC-123" System does is take it a step further to improve your college recruiting success rate. It can also help a recruit and his/her family make a better college decision to avoid having to transfer over lack of playing time or not being the right prospect for that program academically. The system can work for sports at all levels of competition.

Matching System Explanation: The first letter (A)/first number (1) is your analysis of the athletic ability of the recruit with this being the highest grade to provide an immediate impact. The second letter (A)/ second number (1) is the realistic matchup with your university in terms of your chances to have the recruit to commit to your program.

If you have an AF/15 it means the recruit has the impact athletic ability you want for your program, but your chances of getting the recruit to sign with your college are very slim. This can be for a variety of reasons such as academics, school location, position/event, level of competition, coaching reputation, etc. That is the type of recruit you need to likely stop recruiting to not waste time and money. That time and money could cost you a "matching" recruit.

The next row that has a BA/21 would mean the recruit has good athletic ability, and you have a great chance of landing that recruit based on the factors mentioned above. The CA/31 means the recruit is not immediately ready to be a major contributor for your program (probably a books scholarship/preferred walk-on caliber for equivalency sports or preferred walk-on instead of scholarship for head count sports). However, the recruit is a perfect match for your university and may have contributing value his/her junior or senior year with your coaching.

The reason there is no BD/BF/CD/CF/24/25/34/35 in the "ABC-123" system is simple. The coaching time is very valuable for your team and should come first. Recruiting time should always be efficient to better your program. You need someone talented for your team for it to get better or at least a positive walk-on recruit that can eventually contribute. Trying to recruit someone with good or average talent, but with little interest in your program isn't prudent and wastes time.

Being realistic in evaluating the recruits you see along with analyzing how well they best fit into your university will help increase your recruiting success rate. This also best balances the time it takes to be successful in recruiting.

This applies whether you are in a major Division I conference or a mid-major, where the "ABC-123" system works best at matchups. It is a successful way of looking at recruiting, and makes a coach look at more than just athletic ability in building a team. It also maximizes that your time is most productive.

10 Key Matching Factors for "ABC-123" Success

1. Academics–does your school profile work with the recruits?
2. Athletic ability-impact to your program
3. Need for your program-starter or depth
4. Recruit interest in your program-what attracts him/her
5. Amount of scholarship needed (equivalency sports)
6. Your main competitors for the recruit-your level or higher
7. Your relationship to decision makers-especially parents
8. Will club or HS coach help you with recruit?
9. Your school location; chance for unofficial/official visit
10. Intangibles that work best for your program success

Information "Superhighway" for Recruiting

1. Twitter for you and to follow recruit; Facebook checking
2. Preptracker/Google alerts to track recruits daily-gain new recruits
3. Ability to text, email with recruit, parents, his/her coaches
4. Mailings designed more for parents than recruits; "Circle of Influence"
5. Ability to have recruit call head/recruiting coach before 11th grade

NCAA Recruiting Rules Must be Followed-
Can Turn A-B/1-2 into A-A/1-1

Hard work and planning are needed to turn an A-B/1-2 into becoming your signed A-A/1-1 recruit over the favored college. You must follow the NCAA rules in the process or if you are caught violating a rule, then you will lose out on your recruit. You also could possibly lose your coaching job in the process.

The previous recruiting system I utilized provided a financial oversight NCAA compliance responsibility. It unfortunately came into play in 1996 after reviewing the recruiting meal expense reports for the UCLA basketball coaches for official visits with 3 impact recruits.

Monty's Restaurant in Westwood, on the top floor of a major office building where you could see all the way to the beach, was the dinner place to go for top Bruin recruits. Jarren and Jason Collins (A-B/1-2), were 6-10 twins from Harvard-Westlake High School in the San Fernando Valley on their official visits along with a top point guard, Earl Watson (A-1), from Kansas City.[12] They were all there for dinner while the coaches were trying to convince the Collins twins to go to UCLA over likely destination Stanford.

UCLA basketball history would be far different if the Collins twins had gone to UCLA over eventually attending Stanford. That night became a big factor.

The NCAA recruiting rules were slightly different then, but dinner was limited to the coaching staff, administration and an equal number of UCLA current players to the amount of recruits going to dinner (three recruits meant three hosts). When the $1000-plus bill came in, and the names were listed, it didn't match the amount of food ordered on the bill.

This should have been a minor NCAA problem with the normal college compliance results being that the extra players that attended would have to write a check to cover their dinner expenses. Athletic Director Peter Dalis allegedly fired head Coach Jim Harrick over just this incident.[13] The Collins twins went on to great college and long professional

---

12 Sports Illustrated article, April 29, 2013

13 http://www.si.com/vault/1996/11/18/219058/out-to-dinner-out-of-a-job-ucla-fired-coach-jim-harrick-for-lying-about-an-expense-account-meal-was-that-the-only-reason

careers. Jason became the first NBA player to ever admit to being "gay" during 2013.[14]

The lesson is that coaches who want to win in recruiting still need to follow the NCAA rules or problems will occur. Today's top recruits in the Internet world make everything they do in the process that much more visible than it was 20 years ago. Also parents and recruits are responsible for knowing the basic NCAA rules or the recruit can be declared ineligible if he/she is involved in an NCAA violation.

Recruits/Parents: You should work with your club/high school coach to determine your realistic ability for Division I play. This becomes important if you are not receiving initial interest letters or being actively recruited by the time you reach September 1 of your junior year in most sports or after June 15 of your sophomore year primarily in basketball. If you haven't received any type of college interest after 11th grade, then you should take your own initiative if you want an opportunity to play in college.

It is normal in today's recruiting to start receiving letters/notes with biography forms from colleges as early as ninth or tenth grade if you are considered as a potential major prospect. Compare the correspondence you receive with what your main coach believes is your realistic athletic ability. This helps you determine what level of college athletics you are best suited. Some colleges do mass recruit biography mailings but aren't really interested in offering a scholarship. They are more interested in filling their database for you paying for their winter or summer sports camps.

Being realistic is the hardest part for a recruit and sometimes even harder for his/her parents. It is essential in finding the right school. If the schools aren't contacting you, then I suggest you contact the colleges that match your ability. It works best by sending out 10 letters/emails to the level of schools that you like and best fit your interests no later than the end of your sophomore year if you are not being recruited. See what type of response you receive.

Let a school know where they can see you compete during the summer. I suggest you participate in one or two college camps after 9th or

14 "Sports Illustrated" lead article, April 29, 2013

10th grade at schools where you really want to attend. This is where you should receive a realistic evaluation from that college of your ability compared to the competition. You will also get a better idea if a scholarship is possible from that school or what level you can best compete. Even the treatment you receive at the camp should provide insight.

The "ABC-123" system may be designed for matchups for college recruiters, but parents/recruits can look at the matching system the same way in determining the right school to attend. The more college information you have, the better the process will turn out.

CHAPTER 9

My Personal Recruiting Stories

loved that every year was a new recruiting challenge. You had to stay innovative and creative to battle for the top recruits annually or to help a sport improve its recruiting position nationally. I considered recruiting as a 24-7, 365- days-a-year experience.

Nationally, I was likely the first full-time college recruiting coordinator to have never been a former high school/college athlete or full-time coach. I considered this an advantage because I could bring new ideas to the recruiting process by using techniques that involved my background in sports public relations and marketing.

I studied the best teams in each sport to analyze what was important to winning. I also wanted to know what the philosophy/message was that each coach wanted to deliver to his/her team. This was designed so that the coach would trust me to be involved with their recruiting because I was knowledgeable.

I wanted to develop a rapport with our current student-athletes along with future recruits, parents and their coaches where the system I developed would be a factor in the decision-making process. I could get just as excited about our university signing the best volleyball player or gymnast or tennis player as I could about helping land the star recruit in basketball or football.

Selected recruiting stories are provided that can be used by coaches, parents and recruits in trying to look at their own situations in this vital process. Many stories can be related to earlier chapter recommendations.

Certain stories show what can happen when you take advantage of the recruiting resources available.

Basketball Gains the Right Reggie: Reggie Miller

Former UCLA basketball center Brad Wright and I spent time driving out to Riverside Poly High School trying to influence the college choice of Cheryl Miller. She was the franchise female basketball player of the 1980s when recruiting rules were different (she once scored 105 points in a prep game).

Losing Cheryl to cross-town rival USC was one of my greatest disappointments. However, that recruiting time and effort paid off in landing her younger brother, Reggie, the following year. No one at the time dreamed that Reggie would become a UCLA and NBA Hall of Fame player.[15]

Bruin head Coach Larry Farmer wanted another Reggie, Reggie Williams, who was the No. 1 ranked player in the country. He went to Georgetown where he had a successful college and then professional career. UCLA was desperate for a small forward. I told the coaches about Reggie Miller, who was planning to attend Cal State Fullerton because his family apparently didn't want him at USC for men's basketball.

I had learned this information in helping recruit Cheryl. I had watched Reggie play and knew he could help UCLA. The Bruin coaches, with some persuasion, ended up successfully recruiting him. He turned out a better fit than the more heralded Reggie Williams. Miller, who was the No. 11 overall NBA draft pick of the Indiana Pacers in 1987, had a longer and more successful NBA career than Williams, who was the No. 4 overall NBA pick of the Los Angeles Clippers in the same draft.

Sometimes being patient in recruiting can land the recruit the scholarship he/she wants late in the process if a top school doesn't get its top choice. It doesn't always hurt the school if it doesn't get its No. 1 recruit. Reggie Miller will be remembered as one of the best long range shooters in basketball history and a fixture in UCLA basketball history.

---

15 http://www.reddit.com/r/nba/comments/2ejqn3/compilation_of_reggie_miller_stories/

Sometimes No. 2 is Really No. 1: Jackie Joyner-Kersee

Reviewing national recruiting services to see where players are ranked is something important in every sport. At the start of the 1980s, services were limited in women's sports. A women's basketball rating service had center Janice Lawrence (she went on to win an NCAA title at Louisiana Tech) rated as the No. 1 player and a post player from East St. Louis, Ill. named Deborah Thurston rated No. 2.

Unranked was Deborah's high school teammate Jackie Joyner,[16] who was known as a track & field standout at Lincoln HS in East St. Louis, Ill. If she wanted to participate in both sports in college under the NCAA rules, then she had to accept a basketball scholarship. UCLA women's basketball Coach Billie Moore arranged for Deborah and Jackie to visit UCLA together.

The new NCAA rules for women's sports (began 1981-82) allowed for expense-paid campus visits. It wasn't permissible to pay for campus visits under the old Association for Intercollegiate Athletics for Women (AIAW) rules that were in effect through the spring of 1981. I gave Deborah and Jackie their campus tours and knew Jackie was special.

Both came to UCLA, with Jackie becoming a basketball starter from day one. Deborah was a four-year part-time starter (shows that ratings can be inconsistent). Jackie even twice guarded and help beat USC's Cheryl Miller in both games in the 1985 season after redshirting to medal in the 1984 Olympics in Los Angeles (she helped UCLA win NCAA track & field titles in 1982 and '83).

Jackie went on to be voted the greatest female athlete of the 20th century as she won three gold medals and produced several world records in track & field under the coaching of Bobby Kersee, who became her husband.

Getting No. 2 turned to gold, so you never know even today how accurate scouting ratings will be for your program. In-person evaluations work best and it doesn't hurt a recruit to do multiple sports in high school to specialize in one in college (it is rare today to do multiple sports).

---

16 http://alumni.ucla.edu/share/ucla-awards/bio/jackie-joyner-kersee.aspx

Pete Sampras to Pros; Sister Stella to UCLA

I met Pete Sampras when he was a "little guy" at age 13 (about 5 feet, 3 inches then) while women's tennis head Coach Bill Zaima and I were on a home visit in Rancho Palos Verdes to try to recruit his older sister, Stella, to attend UCLA.

You could tell that the Samprases were a special, close Greek family from the visit. The dad told us Pete was going to be an outstanding tennis player someday and he was right. Sampras would become the dominating player in the world of hard court/grass tennis for many years.

Stella came to UCLA and won an NCAA women's doubles title. After college, Stella became a UCLA assistant coach and then became the head coach after Zaima retired. I was so happy when she won her first NCAA title in the later 2000s and a second in 2014.[17]

Pete's name and financial contributions were invaluable to Stella and the program. I loved seeing him when he was able to come to home matches. Stella's husband, Steve, taught me some new recruiting ideas from his Alabama college background and gave me another football team to like.

You can learn so much about a family from a home visit or a campus contact with the family together. It works both ways in making first impressions and is pivotal to the success of both the university and the recruit.

Gymnastics Walk-on to Broadcaster: Maura Driscoll-Farden

Sometimes in recruiting you find a non-scholarship athlete who is so special that the sport is only a small part of her value. I gave a tour to Maura Driscoll-Farden and her family. The family was considering whether to be a priority walk-on non-scholarship gymnast for our program.[18]

I found out the family had the funds to afford out-of-state tuition and they were looking at gymnastics as an avenue for a long-term academic commitment for Maura with a top university. If we could help her to be admitted through athletic admissions and not have to wait for

---

17 http://www.uclabruins.com/ViewArticle.dbml?DB_OEM_
ID=30500&ATCLID=207925501

18 http://youngwomeninsport.com/maura-driscoll-farden/

the general admissions process, then the athletic scholarship offers from other colleges wouldn't be a final decision issue.

Maura was admitted and became captain of the team, plus was an invaluable mentor to the younger gymnasts. After retiring, she became a broadcasting intern for me as a co-host of the UCLA "BruinTalk" cable-TV show, which I produced for 35 years. She has had a long broadcast career first in sports, and now hosting various talk and product shows working out of the Boston area. Driscoll-Farden is a name that has been regularly used in recruiting because of her gymnastics and media accomplishments.

The message is you don't have to be an All-American to play a key role in drawing other recruits to your university and being an invaluable contributor. For parents, occasionally it is better to bypass the full scholarship at a smaller school to pay for the best academic university with athletic resources (if you can afford it). This can lead to the long range success of your young adult as a walk-on where the future is after college sports.

Use Athletic Admissions Wisely for Team Success: Devers, Youngs, Murray

Knowing and utilizing the athletic admissions process wisely is vital to your team success (see athletic admissions chapter). You need to find the right student-athlete who can both immediately impact your program and eventually graduate from your college by working with the athletic admissions unit.

Three of the best in history using athletic admissions are Olympic track & field gold medalist Gail Devers,[19] Olympic beach volleyball medalist Elaine Youngs[20] and long-time professional basketball player Tracy Murray.[21]

My boss, UCLA Senior Associate Athletic Director Dr. Judith Holland, made an admissions-risk decision on Devers. She was a top track & field sprinter-hurdler from San Diego and had good grades, but not the best

19 http://alumni.ucla.edu/share/ucla-awards/bio/gail-devers.aspx
20 http://www.teamusa.org/usa-volleyball/athletes/Elaine-Youngs
21 http://www.tracylmurray.com/

test scores. Still, she came across as someone who was going to be successful in school and life. That admissions decision led to Gail becoming a four-time UCLA All-American. She went on to be a multi-time Olympian and triple gold medalist while graduating.

And then there was the story of Elaine Youngs, one of the best all-around athletes as a high school volleyball-basketball All-American. I met her at El Toro HS in Orange County through a high school visit with women's volleyball Coach Andy Banachowski.

Elaine came from a split family and did not have the academic support that a lot of kids have in high school. Holland again took the risk based on the academic program we had in place. The success of Devers figured in Holland's decision.

Elaine was a volleyball success from day one and also played a year for the UCLA women's basketball team. She was a special player and a fierce competitor. She reminded me of three-time volleyball Olympic gold medalist and former Bruin Karch Kiraly in that both hated to lose.

Youngs helped UCLA win an NCAA volleyball title and reach the NCAA semifinals all four of her All-American years under Banachowski. After college she became the first female player to be both a U.S.A. indoor and beach Olympian. She won a bronze medal with another Bruin, Holly McPeak, in her second of three Olympic Games in 2004. More importantly, she is a proud graduate.

Tracy Murray was even a more challenging academic recruit. Murray was the greatest high school basketball scorer in California history (he once scored 64 points in the California state championship game) and one of the best perimeter shooters for Glendora High School. UCLA wanted and needed him, but his academics were borderline for admission.

I thought of an innovative academic idea to best have him considered for approval by the athletic admissions committee. I had watched how well Tracy came across on a television interview on the local NBC affiliate

My idea was to bring him onto campus and videotape him answering a series of academic and life questions. Then the athletic admissions committee would view him over a television screen. He came across great on camera and was admitted through the support of Holland, who wasn't sure about my idea. Tracy may not have received athletic admission if we didn't do the TV interview and just relied on his paper grades and test scores (he is a UCLA graduate and sports broadcaster today after a long professional basketball career).

My tip to coaches is to make sure you learn the academic background and family history of your impact recruits who may not be the strongest students. This can allow you to show them in a positive light to your admissions committee on their ability to succeed at your university. For parents, if you are aware of an admissions issue, make sure the coach knows any specific reason/background for a weaker classroom or standardized test performance.

Don't Help Your Competition Win: Natalie Williams

Natalie Williams was voted the greatest Pac-10 female athlete of conference's first decade of women's sports. She was the first female NCAA All-American in both basketball and volleyball. Natalie was the leading scorer in the 2000 Olympic basketball finals in leading the U.S.A. to the gold medal.[22]

How she got to UCLA was primarily because USC made a major recruiting mistake for its program that coaches should learn from.

Natalie made her USC official visit in late fall under the guidance of the Trojan volleyball coach. UCLA was co-hosting a basketball tournament in Pauley Pavilion with USC also playing. A USC volleyball coach drove Williams to UCLA to watch the Trojans play because by NCAA rules, the scholarship to play two sports had to be in basketball.

Williams it turned out loved seeing the UCLA facilities and liked the way the Bruin basketball team played. She then decided to make an official visit to UCLA. Williams eventually signed with UCLA because of the USC trip to UCLA, which showed that UCLA had a better history of two-sport athletes and after observing first-hand the better campus facilities.

It meant two NCAA women's volleyball titles, a "Sweet 16" berth in basketball and so much positive publicity around her college and then professional basketball career.

---

22 http://www.wnba.com/history/natalie_williams.html

Coaches should be careful in designing the official visit to not accidentally help the competition, especially if it is in the same locale. For parents, if you are unofficially visiting a city/area with two comparable colleges, try to see both to see the differences. It will help in the future final decision.

Don't Take Children of Athletic Employees for Granted: Ryan McGuire

UCLA athletics had a long-time fundraiser named Ken McGuire. He had a son named Ryan, who was a dominating left-handed pitcher-hitter at El Camino Real HS in Woodland Hills, Calif. I knew a lot about Ken and the family (developing relationships in recruiting) and wanted to help the baseball coach.[23]

I found out it was important for Ryan to know we wanted him for Ryan and not because of his dad or anyone else in his family (his sister, Erin, worked for me in athletic recruiting) who had UCLA ties. He had the ability to go anyplace in the Pac-10 Conference. I assisted our baseball coach, Gary Adams, at the home visit by providing a variety of campus materials that Ken hadn't seen. This included a list of two-way players that developed under our coach and separated us from the other conference schools.

Ryan became a UCLA All-American baseball player and ended up having a long professional career. This included six seasons as a major league first baseman and outfielder. After baseball, he received his MBA from UCLA and became successful in the business world with a great family.

The lesson is don't ever take anything for granted in recruiting or you can lose out on what was expected to be an easy recruit for your program. For parents, there is always something new you can learn about your alma mater or a school you think you know by visiting or having a home visit. Doing your research is so important in making sure you are making the right choice.

---

23 http://en.wikipedia.org/wiki/Ryan_McGuire

Extra Homework When Out Recruiting: Golf

For most summers during the latter part of the 1980s, I would spend two or three days in La Jolla, Calif., helping our women's golf Coach Jackie Steinmann recruit at the Junior World Golf Tournament. I would go into the golf tournament office and be about the only recruiter to write down home addresses of the top recruits in the U.S.A. and outside the country who were playing in the event (both men and women).

I would then go out on the golf course and follow the top women's recruits. I would always wear our school logo shirts to show that we were there and interested. I would help the coach arrange dinner with a senior recruit in the local area near the golf course after the tournament when allowed by NCAA rules. I would then usually go on the local home visits to follow up on the relationship being built in the summer.

The last recruit for the 1990-91 UCLA golf team[24] was our first African-American golfer, LaRee Sugg, of Virginia. I walked the junior world course with her grandfather and then met with them with our coach for dinner because we didn't have the budget in those days to fly cross-country for a home visit. I supported the coach by talking about the diversity on campus and on the golf team. LaRee decided to travel across country and join our team of Californians.

When we won our first NCAA golf title at Ohio State in spring, 1991, I had seen each of the five UCLA golfers at the Junior World event and made home visits or had dinners with each of them and our coach. Christy Erb and Elizabeth Bowman were locals from San Diego, and Debbie Koyama lived closest to campus from Monrovia, while Lisa Kiggens was from Bakersfield.

Those four local players with Sugg won our first NCAA women's golf title in a sudden-death playoff. Sugg made the winning 25-foot putt on the extra hole. After graduating, she eventually went back home and became the senior women's college administrator at University of Richmond.

Make the extra effort to gain new information when you are out recruiting. It can benefit you then and in the future. For parents and recruits, know which schools are out watching your events and show the

24 http://www.uclabruins.com/fls/30500/old_site/pdf/w-golf/2011-12/misc_non_event/2012_WGolf_History.pdf?DB_OEM_ID=30500

most interest. Follow up if you are interested in them and it may lead to the scholarship you want.

Family Legacies Are Important: The Johnson Family

Through my UCLA years, I have been able to associate with some great families and at the top of the list is the Johnson family.[25] I got to meet Olympic track & field gold medalist and former UCLA athlete and student body president Rafer Johnson through my UCLA associations. Over the years, I developed a tremendous friendship with him and his family.

Even more special to me is his incredible wife, Betsy, who is the rock in the family. UCLA almost had a negative relationship with the family over the lack of volleyball recruiting for its daughter, Jenny, who developed into a 2000 U.S.A. Olympian in beach volleyball.[26]

It could have been one of the worst recruiting moves to not have Jenny in our program. You should never underestimate the value of a legacy family. It appeared she was going to UC Santa Barbara, which offered her a full scholarship. Our coaches believed there were stronger impact recruits for the program because we had just won an NCAA title.

Eventually, higher powers got involved and an agreement was reached to have Jenny come to UCLA her first year without a scholarship to redshirt. She would then be given a scholarship for the next four years. I don't think the head coach believed she would turn out as talented as she did, but with the Johnson family motivation, he should have known. She eventually became an All-American and one of the best beach players of all time. She also stayed a Bruin in marriage, having a wedding with former UCLA football standout player, Kevin Jordan.

UCLA track & field didn't hesitate in recruiting NCAA All-American javelin thrower Josh Johnson, who could have been an Olympian without an elbow injury right after college. Jenny is now helping coach UCLA's sand volleyball team, while Rafer is an athletic department advisor and Kevin advises UCLA sports teams in a spiritual capacity. After

25 http://www.spotlight.ucla.edu/alumni/rafer-johns_olym/
26 http://www.uclabruins.com/ViewArticle.dbml?DB_OEM_ID=30500&ATCLID=209413566

graduation, Josh worked in UCLA athletics before moving into his current career in real estate development.

There is usually a lot more than sports involved when you are recruiting a legacy family member to your university. I would recommend taking the legacy recruit if he/she is similar talent with another athlete, because the overall value to your program is greatly enhanced in the long run. For parents who are former college athletes and want their children to follow them to their university, make sure you are realistic about the talent level and then ask for an early recruiting decision by that school.

Turning A-B/1-2 Matchup Into Rare Recruiting Win: Keri Phebus

I enjoyed recruiting battles, especially the rare wins when history wasn't on our side. If you look at the "ABC-123" Recruiting Matchup System, tennis player Keri Phebus was an A-B/1-2 because she had the talent to impact any program. Because her parents had UCLA connections, we had a chance to make it an A-A/1-1 grand slam vs. the college favorite, Stanford.[27]

She is one of the few players in NCAA history to win the NCAA singles and doubles titles in the same year.

I went with UCLA women's head Coach Bill Zaima on the home visit to Newport Beach, Calif. to meet with Keri and her parents. We tried to sell her on how she could come in and play No. 1 singles and doubles for us and Bill could coach her to the maximum of her ability. I tried to explain why UCLA was a better choice than Stanford for her future in tennis and academically because of her interest in communications. The official campus visit gave us a chance.

Keri and I had a two-hour phone conversation on the night she made her decision. My wife was amazed as I paced back and forth in the kitchen walking and talking to her about the key issues. She was leaning to Stanford, but her parents were letting her make her own decision and wanted to see her play.

27 http://articles.dailypilot.com/1999-11-22/news/export65071_1_keri-phebus-corona-del-tennis-courts

She finally told me at the end of the call that she was going to UCLA, but I wasn't sure until she called Zaima. She went on to become probably the best all-around tennis player in UCLA history. Not only was she a tennis All-American, but she was voted into the UCLA Athletic Hall of Fame. After a short professional career, she became a great wife and mother and still is so special for UCLA.

Sometimes if you keep working as hard as you can when you have a solid match based on the "ABC-123" system, then you can build a stronger rapport than your opposition and pull off recruiting magic. The Keri Phebus recruiting win was something I will always remember.

"Circle of Influence" Leads to 3 Basketball Final Fours

Our recruiting system contributed to UCLA making three straight basketball Final Fours in 2006, 2007 and 2008. The key was utilizing what I now call the "Circle of Influence" in assisting new basketball Coach Ben Howland in his first recruiting class. This also included helping recruit future NBA player Ryan Hollins to attend UCLA (the year before Howland became head coach) after he was released from his Saint Louis University letter of intent.[28]

Hollins had signed a letter of intent to play at Saint Louis, but the coach left thereafter for the University of Washington. Saint Louis wouldn't provide him the necessary NCAA release to follow the coach as a freshman, but did give permission for other colleges to recruit him. I knew Ryan was an outstanding track & field jumper and utilized the Bruin track and field coaches to help the basketball coaches because our recruiting needed something extra for closing.

Ryan's dad preferred he stay local for college and so did his Muir (Pasadena, Calif.) high school coaches ("Circle of Influence"). He started in an NCAA basketball title game and helped UCLA beat USC in track & field by scoring key jump points. He then went 100% to basketball and eventually onto a long NBA career.

When Howland arrived at UCLA, I had a meeting in his office. He had an incredible memory for details in the recruiting process. I told

---

28 Los Angeles Times article, May 22, 2002

him that we had strong relationships with three top local recruits and their families from unofficial visits. The threesome could help restore UCLA's Southern California recruiting reputation if Howland could get them—Jordan Farmar, Aaron Afflalo and Josh Shipp.[29]

All were likely going to colleges outside of Southern California. However, their "Circle of Influence" showed local connections or they wanted them to stay local. I gave Coach Howland their contact information and packets of UCLA materials for him to make both high school and home visits.

Howland "sold" all three and remade the UCLA basketball program back into a national power with Final Four appearances in 2006, 2007 and 2008. Other recruits followed such as Darren Collison, Kevin Love and Russell Westbrook to make that possible.

For coaches, you should always start recruiting in the geographic area of your college. Then try to recruit the rest of your state for your biggest advantage over coaches going into your state to take your prospects. You can then expand nationally and only outside the country when you have to.

For parents, there are advantages to looking at your local schools first. Then you can expand your list if the scholarship is not there or you think being further away from home will be a better college experience for your teenager.

Coaching Reputation Can Bring Extra Recruits: Courtney Mathewson

Courtney Mathewson wanted to play college water polo, but was being recruited by some colleges as a swimming sprinter over a strong water polo player. However, I knew her speed would help our water polo program with us having the No. 1 leader in future U.S.A. Olympic gold medalist Coach Adam Krikorian. He was aware of Courtney because of our system of cross-matching multi-sport recruits.[30]

---

29 http://news.google.com/newspapers?nid=2457&dat=20041105&id=BQ40AAAAIBAJ&sji
d=yeAIAAAAIBAJ&pg=1348,1610291

30 http://www.uclabruins.com/ViewArticle.dbml?DB_OEM_
ID=30500&ATCLID=208183417

After seeing her potential talent, Krikorian gave her a small scholarship. It turned out to be one of the greatest moves in women's water polo history based on NCAA titles each season and an Olympic gold medal.

Courtney's most memorable goal came as a sophomore in 2006 with 1 second left to give UCLA a 9-8 upset victory over heavily favored USC for the NCAA title. She will someday be in the UCLA Athletic Hall of Fame for what she meant to Bruin history. This includes winning four NCAA titles, plus being a contributing player to the 2012 U.S.A. Olympic gold medal team in London.

This recruiting showcases the advantage of sharing information with a "TEAM" system. The water polo program may have lost Courtney to another college without swimming first considering her for a partial scholarship because of her sprinting skills and the information being shared. A football/basketball men's sport coach or basketball/volleyball women's sport coach can benefit through the help of other sport coaches for two-sport athletes for example.

Coordinating shared information on multi-sport athletes can be invaluable in your program winning and in possibly finding a recruit that is capable of contributing in more than one sport. For parents, it doesn't hurt your scholarship chances for your son/daughter to contribute to a high school in multiple sports even if there is going to be a one-sport specialization in college.

Coaches Should Know Their Academics in Recruiting: Baseball Pitcher Trevor Bauer

UCLA's John Savage is one of the best all-time college pitching coaches to go with being one of the top head coaches. He is so adept at judging pitching talent that he is the only college coach to ever have the No. 1 overall major league draft pick in pitcher Gerrit Cole and the No. 3 overall major league draft pick in Trevor Bauer, the 2010 College Pitcher of the Year.[31]

Bauer was an honor high school student who was going to graduate a semester early to go to college to begin pitching right away (much more

---

31 http://www.uclabruins.com/ViewArticle.dbml?DB_OEM_ID=30500&ATCLID=208182496

common in football). By doing this, he would eliminate the chance to be professionally drafted out of high school. Coach Savage expected me to work with him to showcase our top academics to help convince Trevor and his parents that we were the right college to receive the best of baseball and the classroom.

Coach Savage had me sit down with Trevor and his father and with a designed academic plan for him to matriculate early into UCLA and immediately contribute to the team. The plan would have his academics moving to a possible early college graduation and then he would move onto a pro baseball career. He enrolled early at UCLA and along with Cole pitched us to the 2010 College World Series, our first appearance in 15 years.

Coaches need to know how their college academics work. They should learn from their academic counselors, school administrators and even their student-athletes because it should be an important part of the recruiting process. The important NCAA statistic is only about 1% of all collegiate athletes have professional sport careers.[32] For parents and recruits, they need to see how academic oriented a coach will be because so few college athletes compete later in life and the degree is paramount.

Recruiting a Whole Family Isn't Easy: The Reeveses Children

Recruiting is something I believe never stops. You need to recruit all family members without making assumptions that a brother or sister will follow another to the same school ("Circle of Influence").

No family gave me more pleasure to recruit than the children of former UCLA women's volleyball and basketball player Jeanne Beauprey Reeves and her husband Mike Reeves (the brother of former UCLA women's volleyball player and assistant coach Lisa Reeves).[33]

---

32 www.businessinsider.com, February 10, 2012

33 http://www.ncaa.com/news/volleyball-women/article/2011-12-16/it%E2%80%99s-family-thing

Relationships are so important in the process and should continue long range. Even though Jeanne also coached at UCLA, there were no guarantees that any of her three children would follow.

The first teenager of the Reeves' children to go to UCLA for volleyball was the oldest son, Connor, in the middle 2000s. He was a walk-on setter who the coaches weren't sure about even though he was a top player in San Diego County. Then came the national recruiting of the talented daughter, Kelly, who had her pick of top colleges as a high school All-American.

Jeanne knew the sport inside and out and wasn't sure our volleyball program was the best place for her daughter. From talking with the administration, I told Jeanne that things would work out for Kelly if she would believe in UCLA. It was a tough decision, but Jeanne decided with Kelly that UCLA would be the place and signed to play.

When the UCLA women's volleyball team won the 2011 NCAA championship with a second-year head coach, part of the tears I had was watching Mike and especially Jeanne celebrating in the stands as Kelly started on the title team. The whole family was together and it made recruiting so rewarding. I helped recruit their final child, Jake, an honor student, to play volleyball at UCLA instead of Harvard. He started a few matches in his first two years as an outside hitter and should enjoy a solid college career.

These types of family relationships don't always happen in recruiting, but this is what I love the most about it. It isn't always easy to get one family member to follow another to the same school, but in this case it worked by treating each family member as his/her own unique person. For parents with multi-college-ability children, you need to decide whether having the family at the same school is a plus or whether you want different places.

Final Advice

You have to consistently work hard and effectively to have long-term success in recruiting. You can't rest on your laurels or with the previous success of your team. Just because something works once, it doesn't always mean it will work a second time, so you have to be adaptable and utilize information to your best advantage.

Coaches and parents should look at these recruiting stories, especially the closing summary, as an opportunity to analyze how they fit into the process. Each sport can be unique in recruiting, but in the end the goal of matching the recruit with the right school is the objective that needs to be met.

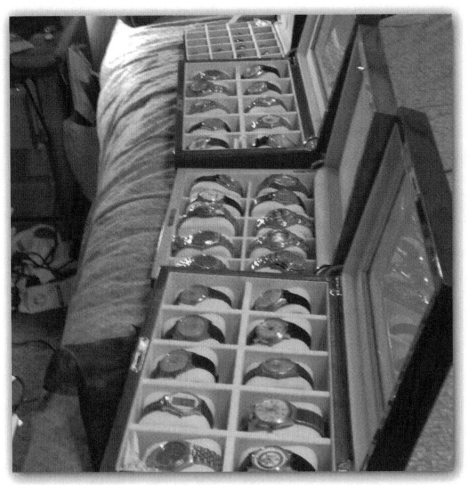

College athletes, coaches and administrators love receiving championship watches or rings for team success. Recruiting is the key.

CHAPTER 10

Taking Advantage of the "Recruiting 101" Blueprint

Recruiting can be a fun and enjoyable experience for coaches, recruits and parents. If a university utilizes the blueprint as directed in this book using the "TEAM" concept, then both coaches and staff can feel part of something special when key recruits decide to attend.

I believe it helps unite an athletic department when the major staff units are part of the same message as initiated through the athletic director. The organization is better and it makes recruits and their families believe they are important when they are given opportunities to interact with more than their own potential team members.

Making official and unofficial visits special helps every aspect of the athletic department when you get the recruit to go to your college. Signing top recruits helps in publicity, marketing, fundraising, weight room, training room and other areas. It also can translate into landing other top recruits because handling the recruiting in a positive way makes families believe your school really understands the process.

For parents and recruits, seeing how organized and united a college is during the recruiting process makes the final decision easier. You feel more comfortable with the college selection. It also helps that you have met and know more people from the campus visit. You believe the school really wants you.

I have found that the more comfortable that recruits/parents are with a program, then the transition from high school to college becomes easier. The recruit is usually more successful starting out in both the sport and the classroom. The parents have fewer worries and issues and are more supportive.

Utilizing Recruiting "Doctor's Chart"

I know it is the computer age and there are a lot of wonderful recruiting programs that chart and encode the information for your sport. However, I still prefer to supplement any computer information by having a paper "doctor's chart" as I call it. The chart should include the biography sheet, plus a sheet of contact/phone-call background to have current data in one place.

The "doctor's chart" should be placed in color-coded folders for your top recruits—different color for senior (blue) vs. junior (gold) vs. sophomore (green) vs. freshmen/younger (red). Any other prospects for that recruiting year are placed in one folder where they can move to their own folder if they move onto your top recruiting list. The prospects are then moved back into the general folder if dropped/recruit goes elsewhere.

The advantages are two-fold. The chart can be reviewed quickly in-house by any coach or key staff member for official or unofficial campus visits (some coaches prefer I-Phones/Tablets/I-Pads, which is fine). Second you keep what is most important on paper in one place where you can take it with you on the road. You may not always have cell/computer reception/access where you can review the notes you have immediately without having to scroll through computer data.

The "doctor's chart" folders move easily from year to year until graduation in a file cabinet and new recruits are added within the system. Old recruits can be archived in case you later recruit a brother or sister or cousin of that recruit so you can review what was done. Everyone has different systems, but this approach gives "TEAM" members access to information if the head coach isn't around for an unofficial visit or you don't have immediate access to the computer materials, for example.

Coaches: A coach should note on the chart when materials are mailed to the recruit and family as well as when the recruit visited the campus or attended a home event. All outgoing phone calls should also be charted per NCAA rules (also include calls the recruit or parent make to you) and the topic of the conversation listed so the next coach that calls has information to utilize. On most recruiting computer programs, you have the same information encoded, but you usually have to move screen to screen. I found it easier to have everything in one folder on a couple of separate pages divided by recruiting graduation years. Every coach operates differently, but this allows your system to be on a computer and via paper in case you don't have the Internet available or your computer system goes down.

Coaches should always ask the recruit/family to respond back at the end of any correspondence (phone, email, letter, in-person contact) as a sign that recruiting is progressing favorably. This is critical and underdone by most coaches. You usually won't win in recruiting if you only have one-way communication. It also builds your trust with the recruit and family.

The message to the recruit can be as simple as sending the school an updated transcript or emailing his/her upcoming playing schedule or a new cellphone number for the club coach, etc. The idea is to make the recruit feel responsible to keep things going in the process. This helps you to win in the end or know quicker when you need to move onto the next recruit because the trust isn't there.

One other area in which coaches could improve is making the initial recruiting phone call more productive. Most coaches over-talk to recruits, thinking they are selling their programs (80% coach talking-20% recruit speaking in the first phone call is average). My research shows that the first call should be about 60%-40% with coaches asking the recruit key questions. You can then better assess the answers for maximum productivity in the process and it more likely allows the recruit to feel more comfortable asking you questions/concerns.

Knowledge is such an important edge in recruiting. Asking questions is the best way to achieve this as opposed to a coach thinking he or she is doing a "sales job" over the conversation.

Dealing With Possible NCAA Violations

Coaches sometimes observe NCAA recruiting rules being possibly violated by fellow coaches while out evaluating prospects. Sometimes the recruit tells you a situation that happened that you believe isn't acceptable. My advice to a coach if you see a possible recruiting violations is to ask the fellow coach directly, "I was wondering how you were able to do 'that' under NCAA rules because my compliance officer told me I couldn't do 'that'."

Most coaches, coach to coach, will admit they didn't have permission, but were guessing it was OK under NCAA rules. If you don't like the answer, then turn to your compliance office for advice and confirmation. However, most coaches I find settle it with each other as they go along as it is usually something minor.

I didn't like seeing possible NCAA violations when I was out recruiting and believe it still goes on today on a small scale. Coaches need to make sure they can handle a possible NCAA violation in some way when they see it so it can be prevented in the future. Don't let recruiting irregularities go without a response that could cost you recruits. It is worth checking out with the compliance office, because occasionally a coach has found an edge in the NCAA rulebook or one conference said something was OK to do that another conference needs to be aware of in the recruiting process.

Parents/Recruits: You usually desire the biggest or best scholarship or at least a top university to attend. Doing your homework is essential to winning in the end with the right college. If your son or daughter is a point guard and the school recruited a point guard the previous year and has another point guard on its roster, it is less likely the college would provide a scholarship to your teenager. However, if a college has a senior point guard and point guard is a priority for recruiting, then it is easier for your son/daughter to strongly consider that school (use the college athletic website to research).

The same goes if you are the goalkeeper in soccer, lacrosse, ice hockey or water polo for example. Need is usually the No. 1 recruiting factor for a successful college team to maintain winning over the years. You need to check what the roster (available on the website) looks like and anticipate team recruiting priorities a couple of years out. If a college currently has a couple of goalkeepers, it probably doesn't need you, but if there is a senior starter, then it is possible.

You must be realistic in assessing what level you can play. Reality makes the recruiting experience much better in finding the right college where you can come in and compete successfully not only in the sport, but in the classroom. The best people to assess your talents are usually your outside club coaches or a coach from another school in your league (get more than one opinion). Second best is summer camps/showcases where you hopefully will have a college coach or showcase coach that will be honest with you about your skill set. It also can help to talk to your guidance counselor or teacher you trust about your academic ability and what type of college they think would be best.

The most important lesson is that going to the highest athletically ranked college in your sport is not always the best decision. Many times it leads to unhappiness and transferring. Sometimes smaller/not as strong athletically, but stronger academically is better. You then have a better chance to come in and contribute and feel more comfortable. Asking questions is critical. Talk to the other student-athletes and their parents and review all aspects of the campus program to make the decision easier. Visiting the campus is always the best way to decide.

Final Comments: This book is innovative and unique in recruiting circles because it provides a recruiting blueprint for coaches, parents and recruits. It also discusses the major aspects of the recruiting process. It covers the important points needed for a recruit to be NCAA eligible for a scholarship and the steps suggested to a college in how to land the best recruits to improve its program.

Both the "TEAM" approach to recruiting and utilizing the "Circle of Influence" concept work. This is not only for the best interest of the athletic program, but enhances the experience for the recruit and his/her parents for both official and unofficial visits. The "College Comparison Chart" is an excellent representation of the factors that should go into the final college decision and what a college should be presenting in the recruiting process.

This book is designed for college programs that want to advance nationally by utilizing the concepts listed in the "ABC-123" Recruiting Matchup System. The recommendations provide a working platform that should allow a sports program to better compete for a higher level of recruit.

For parents/recruits, this book should provide a blueprint for the future student-athlete in finding the right level of college to excel. Also you will be able to effectively ask the necessary questions to conclude if the college is the right match. Is the school offering you the scholarship or just a place on its team or just stalling you in hopes it lands another recruit first?

The different systems in the book and the comparison chart have proven successful over the years to work for both colleges and recruits. You want to see a positive relationship between coach and recruit/parents that can make college the best experience possible and a win-win situation.

It is so important for a coach to be realistic in the recruiting process for his or her chances of success, but even more for the parents and recruits. They have to be realistic as to what level their son/daughter could play so they are looking at the right colleges. This means if it is an equivalency sport, what is the true scholarship value he/she would have to that school? This is based on the quality of the sport and the impact to immediately contribute to that program.

This is always a major challenge and a battle between the bigger schools offering less scholarship money to have an NCAA title contender vs. the mid-majors offering major scholarships to try to improve their programs. Parents have to access what is best for their family financially for the future when this occurs.

The goal of "Recruiting 101" is for readers to take advantage of the blueprint provided. Following the information outlined in the book will assist coaches, parents and recruits for success. The key lesson I learned from legendary basketball Coach John Wooden that I always followed in recruiting was, "failing to prepare is preparing to fail."[34] It works.

---

34 https://www.goodreads.com/author/quotes/23041.John_Wooden

The John Wooden Statue (wife Barbara and son Jeffrey standing) has special meaning because the teachings of Coach Wooden are invaluable in the recruiting process.

20 "RECRUITING 101" BOOK TERMS

ABC-123 SYSTEM: A recruiting letter/number matching system designed to show a recruit's overall athletic talent and suitability for a particular college. The system is designed for a college recruiter to look for the best high school talent combined with the best college that the recruit should attend.

ATHLETIC ADMISSIONS: Each college has some type of admissions system through its athletic department that allows recruits to be admitted to that university. This usually happens earlier than when regular students apply and sometimes without the same type of grades and test scores.

CIRCLE OF INFLUENCE: A recruiting system based on dividing a circle into eight parts that includes various key individuals surrounding the recruit who know and could have influence on him/her on the final college decision.

COLLEGE COMPARISON CHART: An academic, athletic and social/intangibles list that allows a recruit and his parents to compare three colleges among the usual important factors that go into a final college decision.

COMMITTING: A term where a recruit tells a college that he/she has made a final decision to accept an athletic scholarship to attend that school. It can happen anytime an athletic scholarship is offered and usually happens no later than in the 12th-grade academic year.

CONTACT/EVALUATION: When college coaches talk to a recruit/parents in person, it is called a contact; when college coaches watch the recruit play/compete, it is known as an evaluation. The NCAA limits the number of contacts and evaluations by sport with recruits and parents that coaches can utilize.

DEAD PERIOD: The time when a recruit and his/her parents cannot make official or unofficial visits to a college campus and talk to anyone associated with the athletic program. This usually occurs around letters-of-intents, NCAA championships and coaches' conventions.

ELIGIBILITY CENTER/SLIDING SCALE: All recruits must register with the NCAA Eligibility Center while in high school if they want to compete in collegiate athletics. The sliding scale is a combination of academic class grades and standardized test scores where a recruit must predict at a certain combination level in order to be eligible to compete.

FULL/PARTIAL SCHOLARSHIP/COST OF ATTENDANCE: Full scholarships include what it costs to go to school (usually called tuition and fees), what it costs to live on campus (usually called room and board) and what it costs for course-related books (called books). Beginning in 2015-16, colleges will be able to additionally offer funds called the "Cost of Attendance" as listed as necessary school costs to supplement educational, living and books costs in the official university directory. A partial scholarship is any combination of the full scholarship and is almost always found in equivalency sports.

HEAD COUNT/EQUIVALENCY SPORT: Head count sports are where almost all athletes are given full scholarships and schools are limited in the total number of athletes allowed to be on scholarship. Equivalency sports are ones where most recruits receive small scholarships and the total number of athletes on scholarship cannot exceed a number in the sport as determined by the NCAA, but a school can have as many athletes as it wants on scholarships.

IMPACT/5-STAR ATHLETE: The top high school athletes who can have their pick of colleges in their sports are known as impact players or rated as 5-star athletes. There are only a few of this type of recruits in each sport.

JUNIOR DAYS: This is a sports program held at colleges around the country in almost all sports where a coach tries to invite the top juniors in high school to visit to his/her college at their expense to see the campus.

LETTER-OF-INTENT/GRANT-IN-AID: When a recruit decides to attend a college, he/she signs two documents during the senior year. The letter-of-intent is the legal paperwork that binds a recruit to a college. The grant-in-aid is the athletic scholarship paperwork that indicates how much money (from partial to full scholarship) that a recruit will receive. At least one parent must sign each document along with the recruit to make it legal and both documents must be returned to the college within a designated time period to be valid.

NCAA: The National Collegiate Athletic Association (NCAA) is the governing body of almost all of collegiate athletics in the U.S.A. (the

National Association of Intercollege Athletics (NAIA) is a smaller college division). The NCAA is divided into Division I, II and III colleges and scholarships vary by level of play from full athletic to academic only. All scholarship rules and eligibility issues are run through the organization.

OFFICIAL/UNOFFICIAL VISIT: When you visit the college campus and parents/recruits pay their expenses such as parking and food, it is known as an unofficial campus visit (this usually happens between ninth and eleventh grade). The official visit happens when the college pays all of your expenses from transportation to housing to meals and almost always happens in the senior year. A recruit is allowed to take five official visits under the NCAA rules.

RECRUITING SERVICES: Companies that offer parents the opportunity for a fee to promote their sons/daughters to colleges around the country. The service usually provides a video and an information sheet to colleges. Most services are involved with the major sports and some specialize in one sport. They are the most valuable with a family that is not receiving any college recruiting interest going into 12th grade.

REDSHIRT: Under NCAA rules, a recruit has five years to complete four years of eligibility and if he/she misses a playing season because of an injury or doesn't play because of team development, it is known as a redshirt year. This can happen only once over the college playing career.

SIGNING PERIOD: During the senior year the recruit is able to sign athletic scholarship papers to bind him or her to a particular college. There are letter-of-intent times to sign for early scholarships (November most sports), regular (February football) and late (April all sports).

TEAM SYSTEM: Togetherness, Excellence, Achievement and Momentum ("TEAM") are blended together in an athletic department to assist coaches in having recruits attend their schools because everyone is working as a unit for success.

WALK-ON: A recruit who makes a decision to attend a college without the benefit of an athletic scholarship to play on a team. He/she goes through the recruiting process and works with the college to attend in a similar way as the scholarship athletes. Once he or she is there, the recruit is known as a walk-on.

Recruiting 101 Footnotes

1. www.ncaa.org website home page
2. www.nationalletter.org website national letters of intent
3. www.ncaa.org website home page
4. http://www.phrases.org.uk/meanings/big-fish-in-a-small-pond.html
5. www.ncaa.org website home page
6. www.ncaa.org/d1 website
7. www.ncaa.org/d1 website
8. pellgrants.educationconnection.com website
9. www.fafsa.ed.gov website
10. http://web1.ncaa.org/ecwr2/ncaa_ems/NCAA.jsp
11. www.ncaa.org/d1 website
12. "Los Angeles Times" sports article, November 14, 1996
13. http://www.si.com/vault/1996/11/18/219058/out-to-dinner-out-of-a-job-ucla-fired-coach-jim-harrick-for-lying-about-an-expense-account-meal-was-that-the-only-reason
13. "Sports Illustrated" lead article, April 29, 2013
14. http://www.reddit.com/r/nba/comments/2ejqn3/compilation_of_reggie_miller_stories/

15. http://alumni.ucla.edu/share/ucla-awards/bio/jackie-joyner-kersee.aspx

16. http://www.uclabruins.com/ViewArticle.
    dbml?DB_OEM_ID=30500&ATCLID=207925501

17. http://youngwomeninsport.com/maura-driscoll-farden/

18. http://alumni.ucla.edu/share/ucla-awards/bio/gail-devers.aspx

19. http://www.teamusa.org/usa-volleyball/athletes/Elaine-Youngs

20. http://www.tracylmurray.com/

21. http://www.wnba.com/history/natalie_williams.html

22. http://en.wikipedia.org/wiki/Ryan_McGuire

23. http://www.uclabruins.com/fls/30500/old_site/pdf/w-
    golf/2011-12/misc_non_event/2012_WGolf_History.
    pdf?DB_OEM_ID=30500

24. http://www.spotlight.ucla.edu/alumni/rafer-johns_olym/

25. http://www.uclabruins.com/ViewArticle.
    dbml?DB_OEM_ID=30500&ATCLID=209413566

26. http://articles.dailypilot.com/1999-11-22/news/
    export65071_1_keri-phebus-corona-del-tennis-courts

27. "Los Angeles Times" sports article, May 22, 2002

28. http://news.google.com/newspapers?nid=2457&dat=20041105
    &id=BQ40AAAAIBAJ&sjid=yeAIAAAAIBAJ&pg=1348,1610291

29. http://www.uclabruins.com/ViewArticle.
    dbml?DB_OEM_ID=30500&ATCLID=208183417

30. http://www.uclabruins.com/ViewArticle. dbml?DB_OEM_ID=30500&ATCLID=208182496

31. www.businessinsider.com, February 10, 2012

32. http://www.ncaa.com/news/volleyball-women/ article/2011-12-16/it%E2%80%99s-family-thing

Sondheimer utilized working at four Olympic Games to assist his recruiting approach. This picture is with Olympic volleyball announcers Paul Sunderland and Kevin Barnett at the 2012 Olympics in London.

About the Author

Michael Sondheimer spent over 30 years as the Department Recruiting Coordinator for the UCLA Athletic Department. During the Sondheimer recruiting period, UCLA won 70 NCAA titles in 19 sports and 15 sports were ranked No. 1 nationally in recruiting.

UCLA's football teams went to Rose Bowls in the 1980s and '90s as well as other major bowl games. During Sondheimer's work duration, the university produced more Olympians and Olympic medalists than any other college. UCLA also became the first university to win 100 NCAA titles.

Sondheimer developed an "all-sport" recruiting system that was innovative and different compared to other major Division I universities. The system provided UCLA coaches a consistent recruiting platform and a combined information operation for finding and evaluating the best student-athletes across the nation and even outside the United States. It contained a compliance component that limited NCAA pitfalls that coaches can accidently have with regard to campus visits and off-campus evaluations/contacts.

The system included working with athletic admissions and recruit transcripts while having regular interaction and strategy sessions with the coaching staffs to maximize recruiting their top prospects. The "all-sport" system made it easier for parents and recruits to view all aspects of the UCLA program. This included making more effective official or unofficial visits, receiving regular mailings/emails within NCAA rules, plus encouraging website school research. It brought a better college perspective for families and made it easier to make that important final college decision.

Sondheimer's system was advanced in philosophy and execution compared to the competition. The fact he didn't play organized high school or college sports and was not a full-time coach on any level brought a fresh perspective to the recruiting process. He utilized new concepts that separated UCLA's national message to the public, recruits and their families. He did this while overcoming his learning disability that was diagnosed as Asperger's syndrome, an autism spectrum disorder.

Sondheimer loved speaking yearly about NCAA recruiting rules and how to obtain college scholarships at high schools, youth sports clinics, coaches meetings and recruiting service retreats. He wanted to impart recruiting advice at any level from his vast experience in the field. That is another reason why "Recruiting 101" is written to benefit college coaches of all levels, along with parents and recruits.

What Others Say about Sondheimer:

"Michael was so knowledgeable and helpful to me when I got my basketball scholarship to Santa Clara and again so great in advising me as a parent when my son and daughter had to select their colleges." – **Lance Jackson, CEO and Founder of Shotmaster.**

"There is no one I know that is more valuable in the recruiting process than Michael Sondheimer. He is a fountain of information on almost every sport and was invaluable for me as a parent while my son was pursuing college opportunities." – **Tom Feuer, Emmy winning former executive Fox Sports West, current Director, Los Angeles chapter of the Walter Cronkite School of Journalism and Mass Communication.**

"Michael was involved in both recruiting myself and my sister to UCLA and he gave me the opportunity to work for him for three years in athletic recruiting. I have not met anyone who is more passionate and knowledgeable in the college recruiting process." – **Josh Johnson, former UCLA All-American track & field.**

"When it comes to college recruiting, there is no person like Michael Sondheimer. He work ethic is unmatched and he is always available to help coaches, athletes, parents or recruits with his talents." – **Burt Fuller, former international and college head coach and current college and international official.**

"Not only have I known Michael Sondheimer for over 30 years, but I have worked with him and seen the results of his hard work. There is no question that he is a master of recruiting for any sport. He is passionate, imaginative and creative in the recruiting game." – **Colleen Matsuhara, long-time women's college basketball head coach.**

42613926R00065

Made in the USA
Charleston, SC
01 June 2015